PERFORMANCE STANDARDS AND AUTHENTIC LEARNING

Allan A. Glatthorn

EYE ON EDUCATION
6 DEPOT WAY WEST, SUITE 106
LARCHMONT, NY 10538
(914) 833–0551
(914) 833–0761 fax

Library of Congress Cataloging-in-Publication Data

Glatthorn, Allan A., 1924–
    Performance standards and authentic learning / by Allan A.
Glatthorn.
        p.   cm.
    Includes bibliographical references.
    ISBN 1-883001-71-4
    1. Education--Standards--United States.   2. Curriculum planning-
-United States.   3. Educational tests and measurements--United
States.   I. Title.
LB3060.83.G53   1999
371.39--dc21   98-50281
                                                            CIP

10 9 8 7 6 5 4 3

Editorial and production services provided by Richard H. Adin Freelance
Editorial Services, 9 Orchard Drive, Gardiner, NY 12525 (914-883-5884)

Also Available from EYE ON EDUCATION

Performance Assessment and Standards-Based Curricula: The Achievement Cycle
by Allan A. Glatthorn with Don Bragaw,
Karen Dawkins, and John Parker

**The Performance Assessment Handbook
Volume 1: Portfolios and Socratic Seminars
Volume 2: Performances and Exhibitions**
by Bil Johnson

**A Collection of Performance Tasks and Rubrics
Primary School Mathematics**
by Charlotte Danielson and Pia Hansen

Upper Elementary School Mathematics
by Charlotte Danielson

Middle School Mathematics
by Charlotte Danielson

High School Mathematics
by Charlotte Danielson and Elizabeth Marquez

**Data Analysis for Comprehensive
Schoolwide Improvement**
by Victoria L. Bernhardt

**The School Portfolio: A Comprehensive
Framework for School Improvement 2d ed.**
by Victoria L. Bernhardt

Research On Educational Innovations 2d ed.
by Arthur K. Ellis and Jeffrey T. Fouts

**Transforming Schools into
Community Learning Centers**
by Steve R. Parson

Teaching in the Block:
Strategies for Engaging Active Learners
by Robert Lynn Canady and Michael D. Rettig

Encouraging Student
Engagement in the Block Period
by David Marshak

The Paideia Classroom:
Teaching for Understanding
by Terry Roberts with Laura Billings

Research On School Restructuring
by Arthur K. Ellis and Jeffrey T. Fouts

The Educator's Brief Guide to the
Internet and the World Wide Web
by Eugene F. Provenzo, Jr.

Educational Technology:
Best Practices From America's Schools 2d ed.
by William C. Bozeman

School-To-Work
by Arnold H. Packer and Marion W. Pines

The Interdisciplinary Curriculum
by Arthur K. Ellis and Carol J. Stuen

Staff Development: Practices that Promote
Leadership in Learning Communities
by Sally J. Zepeda

Best Practices from America's Middle Schools
by Charles R. Watson

TABLE OF CONTENTS

ABOUT THE AUTHOR

Allan A. Glatthorn is Distinguished Research Professor in Education at East Carolina University, where he teaches graduate courses in curriculum, supervision, and educational leadership. He is the chief author of *Performance Assessment and Standards-Based Curricula: The Achievement Cycle,* also published by Eye on Education. In addition to these works, he has published 20 other professional books. He has been a high school teacher, central office supervisor, and high school principal, as well as a professor at the Graduate School of Education, University of Pennsylvania. He has consulted with more than 100 school systems in developing curricula.

ACKNOWLEDGMENTS

This work has profited significantly from the constructive input of several educators from the Roanoke Rapids (NC) school district who have had successful experience developing and using performance tasks and assessments: John Parker, assistant superintendent; Wilma Falkerson, Manning Elementary School; Ann Hayes, Chaloner Middle School; and Kathy White, Roanoke Rapids High School.

I also feel especially indebted to the external reviewers, all of whom made several excellent suggestions that improved the first draft of this manuscript: Mary Kay Armour, Maryland Assessment Consortium; Debora Silveira, New Paltz (NY) Central School District; and Catherine Thome, Lake County (IL) Regional Office of Education.

Robert Sickles, editor and publisher, first suggested the need for the book and was a constant source of encouragement throughout the process. Finally, my wife and children, as always, provided the understanding and support that extended writing projects require.

Allan A. Glatthorn

PREFACE

This book was written for classroom teachers. It is intended as a practical guide to implementing a standards-based curriculum, developing performance tasks, teaching to those tasks, and using performance assessments. As such it suggests an incremental approach to these goals, helping teachers build from what they already know and do. Rather than claiming that these approaches to curriculum, instruction, and assessment represent a radical paradigm shift, the book presents them as refinements in planning and teaching that any competent teacher can master. For each of the related skills, the book presents a step-by-step approach that teachers are advised to implement flexibly.

The book is divided into three sections. The first section, "Establishing the Foundations," is concerned with the basic understandings. Chapter 1 presents the essential beliefs that inform this work. Chapter 2 explains the key processes that make up the "achievement cycle" and clarifies their relationships. Chapter 3 focuses on the central outcome–authentic learning.

The second section, "Planning for Excellence," explains the four processes that constitute teachers' planning. Chapter 4 explains how teachers can build upon and implement a standards based curriculum. The next chapter is concerned with how teachers can develop long-term plans from a standards based curriculum. Chapter 6 explains how teachers can develop performance tasks and the rubrics needed in the assessment process. The final chapter in this section presents a process for developing units based on performance tasks.

The third section, "Teaching for Success," focuses on the teaching process. Chapter 8 describes "assessment-driven instruction," a process for teaching to the performance task. The next chapter explains how to conduct performance assessments. Chapters 10 and 11 are concerned with providing remediation and enrichment. The next chapter pulls all the pieces together, with an example for each step. The final chapter suggests ways that teachers can continue to expand their knowledge in these areas. The book closes with a glossary of essential terms.

PART I

ESTABLISHING THE FOUNDATIONS

1

UNDERSTANDING THE BASIC BELIEFS

This book is about teaching. It's about a special kind of teaching—teaching that promotes authentic learning, that is based on curriculum standards, and that uses performance assessments to measure student learning. At the outset of such a book, you should know the basic beliefs that undergird this work and reflect on the extent to which they are in accord with your own beliefs.

THE BASIC BELIEFS

♦ Learning is the bottom line.

For years educators have focused on teaching as being the primary concern. They have developed lists of so-called effective teaching behaviors that served as the basis for teacher evaluation and supervision (see, for example, Danielson, 1996). You probably remember the "six-step lesson plan," inaccurately characterized as Madeline Hunter's prescription for effective teaching.

This book is learning centered. It is based on the belief that any teaching method that improves achievement and develops positive attitudes about the subject is an effective teaching strategy.

♦ Authentic learning matters most of all.

As more fully explained in Chapter 3, authentic learning is higher-order learning that is used in solving problems—problems that are meaningful, challenging, and complex. It is often contrasted with standard school learning, learning that emphasizes acquiring information without using it.

Acquiring information without using it to solve problems is like storing vegetables without eating them. However, solving problems without a sound knowledge base is a waste of time, like making vegetable soup without the vegetables.

♦ You matter.

Next to the student, you are the most influential factor in the learning process. As explained below, there are other important factors, of course—but your ability to foster learning and to develop positive attitudes matters most of all.

♦ You are doing something right.

The message of this book is *not* "You are teaching the wrong way, so you must change the way you teach." Furthermore, this book is not about paradigm shifts. Instead, the basic message is this: "Continue to use the methods you have found to be effective, but refine them so that they reflect the best current knowledge about learning."

Do not continue to use methods that have not worked, just because it is more comfortable to do so. Also, do not believe that you have to start from scratch and make radical change.

♦ You need to know two kinds of research—empirical research and experiential research.

The empirical research is what scholars have discovered through carefully designed and implemented studies. The experiential research is what you have learned by being in classrooms 6 hours a day, 180 days a year. Sometimes those two kinds of research are in conflict. When that happens, as it often does, bring your reflective insight to bear. Critique the empirical research with an open and a questioning mind. Analyze your own experiential knowledge with these questions in mind:

• Have the students changed so much that I have to re-think what I know?

- Have the school and community environments changed so much that some of my knowledge no longer applies?

- How sure am I of what I think I know?

♦ You are accountable for the factors you can control or significantly influence—but you are not accountable for the factors that lie beyond your reach.

Consider the factors that influence student achievement, shown in Figure 1.1 (p. 8). That list is a synthesis of 50 years of research on student achievement and can be relied on as a useful guide in thinking about student achievement and teacher accountability. (The factors represent a paraphrase of the research conclusions by Fraser, et al., 1987; the analysis of the degree of teacher control is this author's.)

First, consider the student factors. Obviously, you cannot control or influence student age. You can influence student ability, although some have argued that native intelligence sets limits for what the teacher can do. You can influence student motivation. Because motivation is an internal drive to achieve, you can only establish the conditions that foster that internal drive. One way to increase motivation is to remind students that ability + effort = success.

Next consider the school factors. You can control the quality of your own teaching, although you cannot control it completely. If the school district does not provide quality materials, or if the school does not give you a teachable situation, you probably cannot achieve your full teaching potential. You can, however, request quality materials, rather than waiting for the district to provide you with less-than-satisfactory materials You can control the way you use time in your classroom; however, school administrators control the time assigned to each subject and defend (or fail to defend) instructional time. For those reasons, Figure 1.1 shows time use as influ-

FIGURE 1.1. STUDENT ACHIEVEMENT AND TEACHER CONTROL

Factors/ Control	Can Control, Within Limits	Can Influence	Cannot Control or Can Influence Only Slightly
Student Factors			
1. Age			X
2. Ability		X	
3. Motivation		X	
School Factors			
4. Teaching Quality	X		
5. Use of Time		X	
6. Class Climate	X		
7. School Climate		X	
8. Curriculum		X	
Out of School Factors			
9. Parents		X	
10. Peers			X
11. Use of Time			X

enced, not as controlled, by teachers. You can control your classroom climate, although students can have a positive or negative influence. You can influence school climate, as you work with students and other teachers in maintaining a safe and orderly climate. You can influence the curriculum in a limited sense. Most of the curriculum parameters are set by the state and the district, but you can build upon those curricula by developing effective units of study.

Finally, the out-of-school factors are ones that you can only influence or that lie beyond your control. You can influence parents by helping them become meaningfully involved with the school, although the leadership of the principal and the cooperation of the parents are both essential. You have only very limited influence on peer attitudes and peer pressure. Similarly, you can work with students and parents on how time is used outside of school, but the reality is that students and their parents make almost all the decisions.

This analysis suggests a moderate approach to teacher accountability. It is overly simplistic to examine student test scores and use only those scores to evaluate teachers. On the other hand, it is unrealistic to argue that student achievement should be ignored in determining teacher effectiveness.

You should discuss these matters with your principal and colleagues, to see the extent to which you agree about this key issue of teacher accountability.

♦ Leadership involves the functions designed to help a group accomplish its goals.

It is not the duties assigned to a specific job title. Such functions as the following are involved in the exercise of leadership: helping the group identify their goals; building group cohesiveness; providing resources for the group; and helping the group solve problems. Many staff members can perform those functions—school administrators, central office staff, team leaders, and classroom teachers. Keep in mind some cautions about team leadership. (See Wasley, 1991, for an excellent discussion of "the realities of [teacher leadership] practice.") First, teacher-leadership teams should deal with major areas in curriculum, instruction, the school schedule; and school reform. They should not be burdened in trying to make administrative decisions. They should be provided with the training they need to function effectively as leaders. They should be provided with rewards and incentives that recognize their contributions. Finally, team leadership programs can flourish best in a culture that values collaboration, collegiality, and inquiry.

♦ Usually it's best to work together, but it's all right to work on your own if no one else is interested in working with you.

Two decades of school reform attest to what you have probably learned experientially: school improvement is most successful when administrators and teachers work together in collaborative teams. (See Joyce, Wolf, & Calhoun, 1993.)

♦ Assessment is a critically important part of the learning process, not an unpleasant after-thought.

Assessments should be authentic ones that really measure whether the student has acquired the necessary knowledge and skill—and can apply them in solving problems.

♦ Computers are helpful in facilitating teaching and learning—but they should not take the place of the live teacher.

In the chapters that follow, you will find some suggestions for using the computer, but you should remember that the computer is only a tool for learning. Storing inferior materials in the Internet only results in poor learning.

REFLECTING ON YOUR OWN BELIEFS

You should reflect on your own beliefs about these same issues. The process of reflecting clarifies your beliefs, helps you to understand your own value system, and enables you to openly examine your own experience. You may find the following process useful. First, consider separately each of the issues shown in Figure 1.2 (p. 12). Think about the answer you might give if you were talking with colleagues. Write your answer in a journal. Then reflect about these questions:

- Why do you hold this belief?
- How do you act upon this belief in your planning and teaching?
- How strongly do you hold this belief?

You may wish to share your responses with your colleagues–or simply keep them in your journal. At any rate, you should revisit your belief statements from time to time. Be open to the possibility that your beliefs may change as you get more experience, undertake additional study, and learn more about yourself and your students. Change that comes about as the result of experience with insight is most valuable.

REFERENCES

Danielson, C. (1996). *Enhancing professional practice: A framework for teaching.* Alexandria, VA: Association for Supervision and Curriculum Development.

Fraser, B. J., Walberg, H. J., Welch, W. W., & Hattie, J. A. (1987). Syntheses of productivity research. *International Journal of Education, 11,* 145–252.

Joyce, B., Wolf, J., & Calhoun, E. (1993). *The self-renewing school.* Alexandria, VA: Association for Supervision and Curriculum Development.

Wasley, P. A. (1991). *Teachers who lead: The rhetoric of reform and the realities of practice.* New York: Teachers College Press.

FIGURE 1.2. ANALYZING YOUR OWN BELIEFS

Directions: Consider each belief below. Note one of these as your response.

Y: Yes, I generally hold this belief.

N: No, I don't think I hold this belief.

?: I am uncertain about this belief.

♦ Learning is the bottom line.

♦ Authentic learning matters most of all.

♦ The teacher is the most influential factor in the learning process.

♦ Most teachers only need to refine their teaching knowledge and skills.

♦ Both empirical and experiential research matter.

♦ Teachers should be held accountable only for the factors they can control or significantly influence.

♦ Leadership should be a shared function.

♦ Cooperative problem solving is a good strategy for solving problems, but at times teachers can work on their own.

♦ Assessment is an important part of the learning process, but more use should be made of authentic assessments.

♦ Computers are only a tool.

2

Understanding the Achievement Cycle

You play a key role in what is called here the *achievement cycle*, a systematic approach to curriculum, assessment, instruction, and learning. This chapter defines that term and its related concepts, and suggests how you can use the achievement cycle in your classroom.

CLARIFYING THE ESSENTIAL CONCEPTS

It is essential to understand the key concepts used throughout the book, because several terms are often used in a confusing manner. The important concepts are defined briefly below and explained more fully in later chapters; the glossary also includes a complete list of terms and their definitions.

THE ACHIEVEMENT CYCLE

The achievement cycle, the key concept that informs this work, is defined as the close interactive relationships of four key elements: standards-based curricula; performance evaluation; assessment-driven instruction (ADI); and authentic learning. Figure 2.1 (p. 16) shows the cycle in diagram form.

As Figure 2.1 suggests, the central aim of all curricula, tasks, assessments, and instruction—the contributing components— is authentic learning, which is the central outcome. In general, the cycle begins with curriculum, proceeds to performance tasks and assessments based on that curriculum, and then moves to assessment-driven instruction as the optimal means of accomplishing authentic learning. However, the diagram is also intended to suggest that the contributing elements can be ordered in several sequences, in a recursive manner. Thus, you might begin with assessments, derive the curriculum from them,

FIGURE 2.1. THE ACHIEVEMENT CYCLE

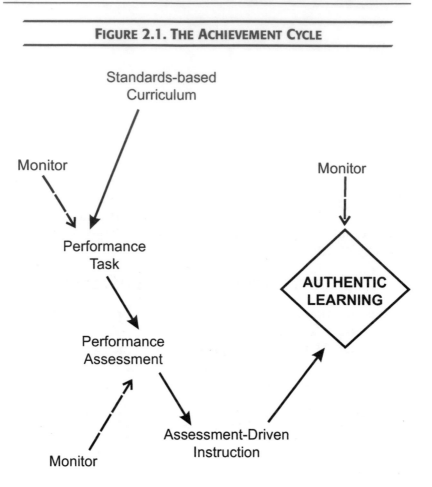

and then move to assessment-driven instruction. The essential element is the congruence of the contributing components and a focus on the learning outcome.

Note also that the figure emphasizes the importance of ongoing monitoring of both the contributing elements and the central outcome. As Palmer (1996) points out, such continuous monitoring is essential if the achievement cycle is to be effective in producing authentic learning. You can do your own monitoring in several ways: observing your students; asking a colleague or supervisor to observe the class; or analyzing results of student performance assessments. This last method is especially important. You evaluate student performance on the task to determine which skills and knowledge require further development. Continuous monitoring using those processes addresses such questions as these: Does the curriculum reflect and embody the best current standards? Do the performance tasks and assessments constitute valid measures of student mastery of the curriculum? Are you devoting sufficient time to teaching to the performance tasks? Do performance results indicate that authentic learning is taking place?

STANDARDS-BASED CURRICULA

Standards-based curricula, as the term implies, are curricula based on content standards as explicated by experts in the field. As Kendall and Marzano (1997) explain, content standards identify what students should know and be able to do; performance standards explicate the level of achievement expected for each content standard. The term content standard or standard is often confused with the term *outcome*. In most usage, a *standard* is a general statement of what students are to learn in one subject by the end of Grade 12. An *outcome* is a more specific statement of intended learning in one year or in one unit. The recommendation here is that your school system should develop its own content standards by drawing from and building on the standards developed by the several professional associations and state education agencies. (See Chapter 4 for a full explanation of your part in the process.)

PERFORMANCE ASSESSMENTS AND RELATED TERMS

Such terms as performance assessment, performance tasks, and curriculum standards are widely used—and are often used in confusing ways. It therefore makes sense to clarify some key distinctions, as the terms are used in this work.

The basic concept is *assessment of student learning*. This is the broad term, to denote the process of gathering data from multiple sources in order to make a judgment about student learning. The assessment process can take many forms, such as observation, interview, discussion, examination of student work and products, test of knowledge, and inspection of student performances and demonstrations (see Linn & Baker, 1996; Chittenden, 1991).

Performance assessment is one type of assessment of student learning. It involves situations in which students must construct responses that illustrate their ability to apply knowledge in completing a complex task or solving an open-ended problem. A fuller discussion of this and related terms can be found in Chapters 6 and 9.

Performance task is a complex open-ended problem posed for the student to solve as a means of demonstrating mastery. The performance tasks constitute the bases for the performance assessment. Marzano and Kendall (1996) identify these defining characteristics of a performance task: requires knowledge to be applied to a specific situation; provides necessary guidance and information to complete the task; specifies learning context (independent, pairs, small groups); and specifies how students will demonstrate their findings or solution.

This endorsement of performance assessments is not to suggest that they are without their own problems. Researchers have noted several limitations of performance assessments in general, especially when used for high stakes accountability. Mehrens (1991) points out that they have difficulty meeting the five criteria of administrative feasibility, professional credibility, public acceptability, legal defensibility, and economic affordability. Gearhart and Herman (1995), note that one difficulty in assessing student portfolios is that the portfolios reflect not only a student's competence but also the amount and quality of support from others, such as teachers and peers. And Guskey (1996) reports on one doctoral study that concluded that the use of performance assessments resulted in only minor changes in the way teachers taught. Teachers interviewed reported that they did not have sufficient training to change their basic pedagogical strategies. Teachers have developed deeply ingrained patterns of instruction that are difficult to change. Systematic training and collegial feedback and support are essential if major changes are to be made in those patterns.

ASSESSMENT-DRIVEN INSTRUCTION

Assessment-driven instruction (ADI) is planning and teaching that are based upon, derive from, and focus on the performance task and its performance assessment. ADI coaches students to prepare them for the performance task and assessment.

AUTHENTIC LEARNING

As noted above, the central purpose of curricula, assessments, and instruction is improving authentic learning. *Authentic learning* is learning that has real-life value, functions as the cornerstone of mastering that subject, and is actively constructed by the student. It is learning that is used to solve problems and complete open-ended tasks. This example illustrates the difference:

- *Standard School Learning:* The students memorize the names of the 13 original states.
- *Authentic Learning:* The students identify patterns of settlement in the 13 states in order to explain where they would have settled if they had been colonists.

Authentic learning is higher-order learning used in solving contextualized problems; it is more challenging and complex than standard school learning. The concept is explained more fully in Chapter 3.

USING THE ACHIEVEMENT CYCLE
IN THE CLASSROOM

In considering how you might best proceed to develop performance tasks and assessments, give primary consideration to taking part in a comprehensive approach that involves the entire faculty. Such a facultywide approach has several advantages: it makes staff development more feasible; it facilitates the sharing of materials; and it is more likely to make a significant impact on student achievement. If a schoolwide approach is not feasible, then consider working with your instructional team. Such collaboration has similar advantages but on a smaller scale. As a last resort, move ahead on your own.

Regardless of how you structure your work, keep in mind the importance of doing quality work. The process recommended in this book is to begin by refining the curriculum for your grade or subject, then designing one performance task and its rubrics. After completing those steps, you can then use assessment driven instruction to help students master the performance task and conclude by making the assessment. Then you can then move to the second task, with greater confidence. Throughout this process, keep in mind the ultimate goal— better learning.

REFERENCES

Chittenden, E. (1991). Authentic assessment, evaluation, and documentation of student performance. In V. Perrone (Ed.), *Expanding student assessment* (pp. 22–31). Alexandria, VA: Association for Supervision and Curriculum Development.

Gearhart, M., & Herman, J. L. (1995). Portfolio assessment: Whose work is it? *Evaluation Comment.* Los Angeles: Center for the Study of Evaluation.

Guskey, T. R. (1996). What you assess may not be what you get. In R. E. Blum & J. A. Arter (Eds.), *A handbook for student performance in an era of restructuring* (pp. IV-8, 1–4). Alexandria, VA: Association for Supervision and Curriculum Development.

Kendall, J. S., & Marzano, R. J. (1997). *Content knowledge.* Aurora, CO: Mid-Continent Regional Educational Laboratory.

Linn, R. L., & Baker, E. L. (1996). Can performance-based student assessments be psychometrically sound? In J. B. Baron & D. P. Wolf (Eds.), *Performance-based student assessment: Challenges and responsibilities* (pp. 84–103).Chicago: University of Chicago Press.

Marzano, R. J., & Kendall, J. S. (1996). *A comprehensive guide to designing standards-based districts, schools, and classrooms.* Alexandria, VA: Association for Supervision and Curriculum Development.

Mehrens, W. A. (1991, April). *Using performance assessment for accountability purposes.* Paper presented at the annual meeting of the American Educational Research Association, Chicago.

Palmer, J. (1996). Integrating assessment and instruction: Continuous monitoring. In R. E. Blum & J. A. Arter (Eds.), *Student performance assessment in an era of restructuring* (pp. IV-6-1-6). Alexandria, VA: Association for Supervision and Curriculum Development.

3

FOCUSING ON
AUTHENTIC LEARNING

You know that learning is central—and you probably are doing a good job of fostering student learning. Even good teachers, however, can refine their teaching. One useful way of refining your teaching is to emphasize authentic learning. As defined previously, *authentic learning* is learning that has real-life value, that functions as the cornerstone of a school subject, and is actively constructed by the student. It involves acquiring a deep knowledge base and using that knowledge to solve meaningful problems. This chapter deals with several related issues: an analysis of the nature of authentic learning; a discussion of the learner's and teacher's responsibilities; a caution about misusing authentic learning; and suggestions for refining your teaching so that authentic learning is more likely to result.

THE NATURE OF AUTHENTIC LEARNING

Authentic learning is perhaps best understood if contrasted with standard school learning, what many teachers have been emphasizing for many decades. The contrasts of these two approaches to learning are shown in Figure 3.1 (p. 26). (The key elements of authentic learning have been derived from the literature, chiefly Brooks & Brooks, 1993; Marzano, Pickering, & McTighe, 1993; and Newmann, Secada, & Wehlage, 1995.) As Figure 3.1 suggests, authentic learning is higher-order learning that is used in solving problems that are presented in their context. It is more challenging and complex than standard school learning. The two approaches to learning differ in several different ways, as explained below.

FIGURE 3.1. AUTHENTIC LEARNING AND STANDARD SCHOOL LEARNING

Aspect	Authentic Learning	Standard School Learning
Problems	Focuses on problems that are open-ended, complex, situated, real life.	Emphasizes problems that involve single answer, simple questions presented out of context; without context; problems seem contrived, unreal.
Materials	Uses multiple materials that provide depth, emphasizing primary sources.	Uses a single superficial text, relying on secondary sources.
Curriculum	Is based on a curriculum that emphasizes major concepts, useful strategies; provides for depth.	Is based on a curriculum that emphasizes facts, formulas.
Assessment	Assesses learning through authentic performance emphasizing the demonstration of knowledge.	Uses short answer tests that focus on memory, comprehension.
Teaching	Requires different approach to teaching: emphasizes higher-order thinking skills; provides scaffolding; facilitates metacognition; uses group dialog; values in-depth learning.	Uses traditional model: teacher explains, students listen; stresses lower order thinking skills; relies upon teacher directed activities; is not concerned with metacognition; uses "busy work" instead of dialog; values coverage.

THE TYPES OF PROBLEMS PRESENTED TO THE STUDENTS

Authentic learning is developed by working on complex problems that usually do not have a single correct answer, but instead involve multiple interpretations and explanations. The problems are presented in context with explanations of who, what, where, and when, and they deal with real-life situations.

Here are two examples:

- Authentic Problem

  Using your knowledge of our school and the problem-solving process, identify one major problem requiring the principal's and teachers' attention. Explain how you think the problem can best be solved, using whatever communication medium that you think would best get your message across.

- Standard Problem

  Write a 500-word theme on this topic: "How we can improve our school."

THE QUALITY OF THE LEARNING MATERIALS USED

If learning is to be authentic, it should be based on diversified learning materials that provide for depth of study and, whenever possible, the use of primary sources. (Primary sources are the original materials, such as newspaper and diaries written at that time; secondary sources, such as textbooks, describe and use primary sources.) Because school textbooks are written for a mass market, most treat a topic superficially. In searching for primary sources, remember to teach students how to access sources through the Internet—the Smithsonian, for example, has an excellent Web site that students can use profitably.

Here is an example illustrating the importance of learning materials. Most high school American history textbooks devote a few pages to the contributions of African Americans, giving special attention to such major figures as George Washington Carver, Malcolm X, Martin Luther King, and Langston Hughes. While those individuals are surely important, they are often represented as historic figures who acted alone. On the other hand,

Dick Russell's recent book *Black Genius and the American Experience* (New York: Carroll & Graff, 1998) devotes a chapter to Wynton Marsalis, showing how he was influenced by Duke Ellington and Ralph Ellison. Suppose you wanted students to solve this problem: "How do minorities influence the dominant culture?" You would be wise to have students use the Russell book instead of the history text.

THE QUALITY OF THE CURRICULUM

The third key component of authentic learning is that it is based on and derived from a quality curriculum. Authentic learning is more likely to occur if the required curriculum is characterized by these qualities:

+ It is based on and derived from quality standards.
+ It emphasizes depth of learning, not coverage.
+ It values generative knowledge—knowledge that is used in solving problems.
+ It makes specific provisions for flexible implementation, so that the teacher can enrich it, make it meaningful to the students, and respond to the special needs of the students.

If the curriculum emphasizes the coverage of too much content, values only the comprehension of facts and formulas, and tries to control teaching completely, then authentic learning is very unlikely to occur.

Consider, for example, two curricula in U.S. history. The traditional curriculum guide covers all the periods, Presidents, major figures, battles, elections, and trends from 1600 to 1990. A quality curriculum that encourages authentic learning focuses instead on four to six major periods, with significant themes interwoven through each. For example, a fifth grade curriculum might emphasize throughout the year the theme of democratic decision-making, as a means of giving some coherence to the subject. Also, the selectivity is more likely to result in deep learning.

In judging curriculum quality, you cannot always rely on the correspondence of the district guide with state standards. In a review of state curriculum standards, three experts gave them an overall grade of D+ (Finn, Petrilli, & Vanourek, 1998). Because you are required to implement the district curriculum, your best response, when working with a required curriculum that seems deficient, is to teach the main concepts and skills while adding elements that will strengthen the district guide.

THE NATURE OF THE ASSESSMENT

Authentic learning is more likely to occur if it is based on a challenging performance task and measured by an authentic performance assessment. Authentic performance assessments have several features that distinguish them from traditional tests (Gooding, 1994):

+ They assess student learning over an extended period of time.
+ They include knowledge and skills needed for success outside of school.
+ They are based on standards and criteria known in advance by students and parents.
+ They are nonbiased with respect to students' learning styles, backgrounds, and ethnicity.
+ They require the use of generative knowledge, requiring students to use knowledge in solving problems and completing performance tasks.
+ They are process-oriented, requiring a performance or demonstration.
+ They are student oriented, involving students in self-assessments.

Here, for example, is a performance task that would be evaluated by a performance assessment in science.

Pretend that you are a water quality technician at the waterworks. Choose the appropriate measuring instrument from your station to measure 50 milliliters of water from the pan of dirty water at the supply station. Draw a picture of your measuring instrument showing the dirty water inside and the marks that indicate that you have 50 milliliters. Choose any equipment from the supply station that will enable you to clean the dirt from the water. Draw a picture showing how you set up your equipment. Report how your experiment works.

Short-answer tests are easier to grade, but they are a poor measure of real learning.

THE QUALITY OF INSTRUCTION

Teaching for authentic learning is recognizable in several ways. First, the teacher values in-depth learning that uses knowledge to solve problems. As a consequence, the teacher emphasizes higher-order thinking, stressing such objectives as these: explain; organize; interpret; evaluate; synthesize. The teacher expects the students to provide elaborated responses. Rather than expecting one-word answers, the teacher probes for more detailed explanations, helps the students develop the skills of representing knowledge visually, requires longer responses, and listens patiently while students struggle towards fluency.

Throughout the lesson and the unit, the teacher encourages students to think about their thinking, using what the experts call *metacognition*. The teacher prompts with such metacognitive questions as "Why did you choose that particular strategy?" and "What were you thinking when you began the story?"

Scaffolding is also important to the teacher and the students. *Scaffolding* is a metaphor for appropriate support. As workers erect a wall, they use scaffolding until they can take it down. A teacher who uses scaffolding gives students the structure they need to solve problems and then systematically removes it so that students can become more independent in their problem solving. At the start of the unit, for example, the teacher explains to the students how they can organize knowledge by using a matrix; at the end of the unit, the teacher encourages students to use their own organizing strategy.

Finally, in observing a classroom where authentic learning is taking place, you would see much cooperative learning and group dialog. Such group work, of course, is task-focused, but quietness and passivity are not encouraged.

Authentic Learning: A Shared Responsibility

Too much educational discourse emphasizes the role of the teacher in the learning process: "This is what teachers have to do." In fostering authentic learning, it makes more sense to see learning as a shared responsibility. In helping students understand this concept, Figures 3.2 (p. 32) and 3.3 (p. 33) are useful. You should feel free to simplify the process shown in Figure 3.2 for younger students. You should also give students all the help they need in using the process. One way to do this is to put a simplified version on the bulletin board and point to the steps as students move through them.

Notice that the emphasis is first on learning, not teaching; what the student does is considered the priority issue. While the model in the form used here suggests a linear process, it is in reality more recursive and interactive—the learner jumps around, skips steps, and comes back to earlier moves.

Throughout the Learning Experience

Throughout the learning experience, the learners contribute to a supportive classroom environment, keep a focus on learning, and motivate themselves to accomplish the learning task. They continuously monitor their learning and the processes they are using, cooperate with the teacher and their peers, and keep in mind the nature of the performance assessment. They are aware of feelings and work to develop positive attitudes towards the learning process.

The Steps in the Learning Process

The learners work their way flexibly through a learning process, beginning with a meaningful goal. They activate their prior knowledge. More important, they acquire new knowledge in an active processing manner: they organize it with their own strategies and they construct their own meaning, drawing pictures and images of the new knowledge. A key step is reconceptual-

---

Figure 3.2. Authentic Learning:
Learner Responsibilities

Throughout the learning experience…

+ I help make the environment one that supports learning.

+ I attend to the learning focus and am motivated to learn.

+ I monitor my own learning, reflect about my learning processes, and am sensitive to my feelings as I learn.

+ I cooperate with the teacher and other learners.

+ I keep in mind the way my performance will be assessed.

+ I value learning: I am aware of feelings and develop positive attitudes towards learning.

I take these steps as I learn…

+ I set a meaningful learning goal.

+ I call to mind what I already know, by activating prior knowledge.

+ I acquire new knowledge in depth:
  - I organize it.
  - I explain it to myself and make my own sense of it.
  - I draw pictures and images of it.
  - I build it into what I already know, reconceptualizing my knowledge.

+ I communicate my new knowledge in elaborated fashion, discussing concepts and sharing ideas.
  - I write about it with full details and illustrative examples.

- • I draw pictures, diagrams, and schematics representing the knowledge.
- • I use metaphors and analogies.
- ♦ I acquire and apply a learning strategy.
- ♦ I use the knowledge and the strategy to work with others in solving a meaningful problem.
- ♦ I evaluate my solution.
- ♦ I demonstrate and share my knowledge.

FIGURE 3.3. AUTHENTIC LEARNING: TEACHER RESPONSIBILITIES

Throughout the learning experience the teacher...

- ♦ Models reflection and insightful thinking and monitors his or her own learning.
- ♦ Helps make the environment one that supports learning.
- ♦ Provides the scaffolding and structure that students need at that time.
- ♦ Helps students work through the steps in the learning experience.
- ♦ Develops and uses quality performance tasks to assess student learning.
- ♦ Welcomes and uses feedback from students about the teaching/learning experience.
- ♦ Is sensitive to and responds appropriately to the affective dimensions of learning.

---

izing their prior knowledge in light of new knowledge that they have actively processed.

One of the crucial steps often overlooked in the learning process is communicating the new conceptualization by elaborating on it. The elaborations (providing full written details, giving examples, drawing visual images, and using metaphors and analogies) are ways of representing the knowledge. If students cannot represent their new knowledge, they have not fully understood it.

In the process of solving problems, the student probably uses a learning strategy. A learning strategy is defined here as a sequence of mental operations useful in solving problems. Some strategies are generic and can be useful in several subjects, as for example:

> Use a matrix to organize information

Some strategies are subject specific, such as this one in mathematics:

> Identify the known elements of the problem.

The process moves to its conclusion: solving a problem in a social context; evaluating that solution; and communicating and demonstrating that knowledge.

With the learning model clarified, it is then a relatively simple matter, as suggested by Figure 3.3, to identify what the teacher needs to do to make that learning process happen.

The model presented here is not prescribed as the best way to teach, and it should not be used to evaluate your teaching. However, you might find it helpful in working with colleagues in a peer-coaching mode, giving one another feedback about your use of the model.

PRECAUTIONS IN USING AUTHENTIC LEARNING

Teachers can misuse authentic learning, with the students learning less as a consequence. The following discussion about precautions is organized around the principles of authentic learning.

AUTHENTIC LEARNING IS AN INDIVIDUAL MATTER

While certain forms of instruction are described as *individualized*, in a true sense, learning always occurs within the individual. As a collection of individuals, groups may show change in their behavior as well, but that change is also the sum of individual growth. This first principle, therefore, reminds teachers that even as they appropriately make use of cooperative learning groups, they should be concerned with the achievement of individual students. Slavin (1990) emphasizes the importance of individual accountability when using cooperative learning. Gearhart and Herman (1995) conclude from their research that the quality of student work reflects not only an individual student's competence but also the amount and quality of assistance received from other students.

Teachers can use several strategies in assessing individual learning when using cooperative learning. First, they can structure group tasks so that each member of the group has a piece of the task to accomplish, relying on peer pressure to ensure that each individual task is accomplished. Second, they can monitor group work closely to observe whether all individuals are actively on task. They can also compute the group score as a sum or average of individual scores, as used in Student Team Learning models of cooperative learning. Finally, they can develop structured systems that enable the members of a cooperative group to evaluate each other's contribution.

AUTHENTIC LEARNING REQUIRES THE ACQUISITION AND USE OF NEW KNOWLEDGE

This principle reminds teachers that authentic learning can take place only when students access new knowledge and use that new knowledge to expand, replace, or deepen existing knowledge. In too many instances, teachers ask students to solve problems simply by brainstorming, without providing a sound knowledge base. Thus, if you ask students to solve a problem of community pollution without adequate scientific knowledge, their solutions are very likely to be flawed.

This principle has several implications for the teacher in fostering authentic learning. The teacher should:

- Identify essential knowledge in the curriculum project, focusing on those central concepts and processes that are vital to understanding that discipline.
- Ensure that assessments require a sound knowledge base.
- Structure the unit so that the design includes knowledge acquisition.
- Enable students to access new knowledge, avoiding the teacher lecture as the least effective means.
- Monitor throughout the unit the students' understanding of the new knowledge.

AUTHENTIC LEARNING REQUIRES REFLECTIVE DIALOG

This principle embodies two closely related components of authentic learning—reflection and discussion. Learning at its best involves reflection about experience—thought that deepens insight. And individual insights need to be tested and shared in group dialog. In too many instances, the class is a busy active place of "buzzing confusion," where reflection is difficult.

One process that seems to work well in fostering reflective insight is the following:

- Model reflection as you teach, by thinking aloud and emphasizing the importance of reflection.
- In class discussions, slow the pace and increase the wait time. After asking a question, wait at least three seconds before calling on a student or asking for volunteers.
- In examining complex questions, ask the students to reflect individually before using group or class discussion. It helps to have students write their answers to complex questions, because the writing process enables them to bring knowledge to the forefront of consciousness and to discern what they know.

♦ Teach students how to reflect in small groups: taking turns; listening actively; sharing ideas; being open to and resolving constructive differences; learning from and giving to others.

AUTHENTIC LEARNING IS MORE THAN ACTIVITY

Many teachers seem committed to "activity-itis," asking students to engage in activities that are unrelated to the learning goal. For example, teachers who think of themselves as innovative often use role playing as a means of teaching concepts, when it is designed primarily to help the role player empathize with others.

Teachers can apply this principle of authentic learning in several ways. In designing units, they can emphasize learning outcomes, not activities. In planning individual lessons, they should ensure that each planned activity relates to the instructional objectives. In teaching lessons, they should operate flexibly while keeping their sights on the learning goal. Finally, teachers should make the learning purpose of each instructional activity clear to students.

AUTHENTIC LEARNING REQUIRES FEEDBACK

All learning requires feedback. The sources can be several: self; the teacher; parents; peers; the computer; external judges; tests. Sometimes the feedback is positive: right; correct; good work; excellent analysis; objective achieved. Sometimes it is negative: wrong; incorrect; not up to standard; poorly phrased; objective not achieved. Although most teachers seem to avoid giving negative feedback, it can be useful if delivered in an objective and constructive manner. Good and Brophy (1991) note that praise, by contrast, can be counterproductive if it seems manipulative or excessive.

Authentic learning is more likely to take place if the feedback is characterized by these features:

♦ The feedback is timely, delivered as soon as possible after the performance.

♦ The feedback is primarily objective, based upon clear criteria and specific evidence.

+ The feedback is multiple, using several sources.
+ The feedback is constructive, emphasizing both the strengths demonstrated and the aspects that can be improved.

AUTHENTIC LEARNING IS BOTH AFFECTIVE AND COGNITIVE

The pressure for teacher accountability as measured by test scores seems to have led many teachers to ignore the affective components of the learning experience. However, rather than returning to the move of the 1960s to isolate affective education, teachers should understand that the affective and the cognitive are closely and perhaps inextricably related to each other, and that in many cases, the affective element is more important than the cognitive one. Consider, for example, the importance of this affective outcome: enjoy reading. Surely nothing is more significant; yet that goal is often ignored.

This principle has several implications:

+ Take time to increase the motivation to learn, emphasizing the meaningfulness of the learning experience.
+ Be sensitive to students' feelings. Know when to ignore them and when to deal with them.
+ Take cognizance of the fact that many students have negative attitudes about schooling, testing, and the subjects they study. Acknowledge those attitudes without capitulating to them. Build positive attitudes by making it possible for students to achieve earned success.
+ Demonstrate positive attitudes yourself and manifest legitimate enthusiasm. Show that you care about the students and value what you are teaching.
+ Realize that what is learned always goes beyond what is tested. Even the best performance assessments measure only a part of what has been learned. And often the part that is not measured is the most important goal of all, such as the following:

- Develop positive attitudes towards mathematics and enjoy solving mathematical problems as a way of increasing knowledge.

REFINING YOUR OWN TEACHING

If you believe that authentic learning is a valuable goal for your students and you would like to refine your teaching so that it is more likely to foster such learning, there are two ways to proceed. One way is to embark upon a program of comprehensive change, using this book as a guide for developing new approaches to all the elements of the achievement cycle. That comprehensive process can work well only if certain conditions are present. First, you need supportive leadership, from the superintendent and the principal. Second, you need colleagues who can work with you, sharing their expertise and knowledge. Finally, you need adequate resources, especially ample time for quality work. Schools that have successfully used performance tasks have found that providing teachers with additional planning time and employing teachers in the summer are effective strategies for supporting teacher planning.

The second way is an individualized step-by-step approach based on a process of incremental change. Identify a unit that you have taught and found generally successful. Check to be sure that it is based on and derived from the current curriculum. Develop a performance task for that unit. Implement the unit, using the new model of teaching. Then conduct the performance assessment. Reflect about what you have learned. Then take a second unit, following the same steps. Again, evaluate and reflect. Continue that process until you have transformed an entire course.

Even though this incremental process does not require you to work with a colleague, you should find collegial interaction and support are very helpful. If two of you can work together in this manner, you should find that you are getting better results than if you worked alone.

REFERENCES

Brooks, J. G., & Brooks, M. G. (1993). *In search of understanding: The case for constructivist classrooms.* Alexandria, VA: Association for Supervision and Curriculum Development.

Finn, C. E., Jr., Petrilli, M. J., & Vanourek, G. (1998). *The state of state standards.* Washington, DC: Fordham Foundation.

Gearhart, M., & Herman, J. L. (1995). *Portfolio assessment: Whose work is It? Issues in the use of classroom assignments for accountability.* Los Angeles: Center for the Study of Evaluation.

Good, T. L., & Brophy, J. E. (1991). *Looking in classrooms* (5th ed.). New York: Harper Collins.

Gooding, K. (1994, April). *Teaching to the test.* Paper presented at the annual meeting of the American Educational Research Association, New Orleans.

Marzano, R. J., Pickering, D., & McTighe, J. (1993). *Assessing student outcomes.* Alexandria, VA: Association for Supervision and Curriculum Development.

Newmann, F. M., Secada, W. G, & Wehlage, G. G. (1995). *A guide to authentic instruction and assessment.* Madison, WI: Wisconsin Center for Educational Research, University of Wisconsin-Madison.

Slavin, R. E. (1990). *Cooperative learning: Theory, research, and practice.* Englewood Cliffs, NJ: Prentice Hall.

PART II

PLANNING FOR EXCELLENCE

4

BUILDING ON A STANDARDS-BASED CURRICULUM

All your planning and teaching will be more effective if they are built on a foundation of a standards-based curriculum. This chapter explains the nature of a standards-based curriculum and emphasizes the key role that you play in making such a curriculum come alive. Even though some teachers believe that they are not responsible for curriculum development, the position advanced here is that, even with state- and district-developed curricula, you and your colleagues are the key actors in the real curriculum that is delivered day by day.

UNDERSTANDING A STANDARDS-BASED CURRICULUM

Your school system is probably expecting you and your colleagues to follow a curriculum based on standards. Almost every state department of education has adopted a set of standards for each subject. And every professional organization has published its own list of standards for that subject. While there are some minor differences between these various sources, the *standards* usually specify what students are expected to learn in one subject after 12 years of schooling. Here are some examples of these standards. (The examples are paraphrased from an excellent compilation by Kendall & Marzano, 1997.)

- *Science*. Understands basic features of the earth.
- *History*. Understands family life now and in the past.
- *Language Arts*. Demonstrates competence in speaking and listening.

- *Arts*. Understands the visual arts in relation to history and cultures.
- *Mathematics*. Uses a variety of strategies in the problem-solving process.

As is evident from these examples, the standards are very general statements of learner outcomes.

Each standard is then analyzed into its related *benchmarks*, the more specific components. Here, for example, are the benchmarks suggested in Kendall and Marzano for grades 3 to 5 for the science standard noted above (paraphrased from Kendall & Marzano, 1997, p. 71):

- Understands the basic features of the earth:
  - Knows that water can change from one state to another through various processes.
  - Knows the major differences between fresh and ocean waters.
  - Knows that clouds and fog are made of tiny droplets of water.
  - Knows that air is a substance that surrounds us, takes up space, and moves.
  - Knows that night and day are caused by the Earth's rotation on its axis.
  - Knows that the Sun provides the light and heat necessary to maintain Earth's temperature.

In some curricula, the benchmarks are stated for a group of grades (such as Grades 3–5); in others, for a specific grade (such as Grade 4).

Each benchmark in turn can be analyzed into its component classroom learning objectives. These are the very specific outcomes that you identify as you plan a particular lesson. The term *classroom learning objectives* is used here with this meaning: specific learner outcomes, derived from benchmarks, used to facilitate the classroom learning processes.

To understand the relationship of benchmarks and classroom learning objectives, consider this benchmark for high school science, from Project 2061 (1993).

> Knows that earthquakes often occur along the
> boundaries between colliding plates.

That benchmark should be further analyzed into its component
classroom learning objectives:

- Define *earthquake.*
- Explain the causes of earthquakes.
- Explain *Richter Scale* as an earthquake measure.
- Explain how earthquake-prone areas can best pre-
  pare.
- Explain what residents should do when an earth-
  quake occurs.

Most teachers prefer to identify such objectives later on, as
they develop their lesson plans. Identifying such objectives too
early in the process might restrict your ability to respond to students' emerging needs or inhibit your creativity.

UNDERSTANDING THE TEACHER'S ROLE

If standards are identified by states, professional groups,
and school districts, what is left for the teacher to do? The answer is, "Carry out many important processes." To understand
how crucial you are as a curriculum worker, consider the teacher functions shown in Figure 4.1 (p. 48). As the figure indicates,
the teacher makes the written curriculum really come alive.

The functions, as listed in Figure 4.1, are used to organize the
rest of this book, explaining each function in the order listed in
the table—except for the evaluation function, which is treated in
all appropriate chapters.

Note, however, that you should use the functions flexibly, in
any order that works for you. There is no right sequence. For example, some teachers have found it effective to start with a unit
that they have previously developed and then find the benchmarks that the unit seems to address. Others identify the performance tasks that they then fit into a long-term plan. It is wise to
read the chapters in the order shown in the table of contents—
and then decide what sequence to follow.

FIGURE 4.1. TEACHER'S ROLE IN A
STANDARDS-BASED CURRICULUM

(The following list of functions assumes that the state or school district has identified the curriculum standards.)

♦ Identify benchmarks for a specific grade level.
♦ Analyze standards and benchmarks to tentatively identify the unit titles.
♦ Develop long-term plans for teaching.
♦ Design performance tasks and rubrics.
♦ Develop units based on performance tasks.
♦ Implement units with assessment-driven instruction.
♦ Conduct performance assessments.
♦ Remediate learning as required and provide enrichment when appropriate.
♦ Evaluate all materials, providing feedback for improvement.

IDENTIFYING THE BENCHMARKS

If your state department of education or your school system has identified specific benchmarks for each grade, then you can move to the next step in the curriculum process, as explained in the following chapter. However, if the curriculum guide has specified benchmarks for only a group of grades, then you and your colleagues need to decide which benchmarks should be allocated to each grade. The following discussion explains one process you can use.

♦ Keep in mind the importance of depth of learning.

Here is an example of why depth matters. F. James Rutherford, director of the widely respected science project, Project 2061, determined that high school biology texts included 120 different technical terms related to the cell—although he and his colleagues decided that only 11 were sufficient (as reported in U.S. Department of Education, 1995). A teacher who tried to cover all 120 terms would find that students probably remembered none.

♦ Estimate how many benchmarks you and your colleagues should try to teach each year.

Here are some guidelines provided by the experts (see Marzano & Kendall, 1996; Kendall & Marzano, 1997; Gandal, 1995; and Glatthorn, 1998).

- The standards-based curriculum should not require more than 80 percent of the total time available, to allow time for enriching the curriculum and remediating learning.

- For each standard, an average of three benchmarks each year seems feasible. Because most curricula are based on 8 to 12 standards, you might consider aiming for 24 to 36 benchmarks.

- For the most part, benchmarks should be allocated evenly from grade to grade, although a larger number may be assigned to higher grades.

♦ Review the content emphases for each grade level.

For many subjects, the curriculum emphasizes particular content to be studied for a given grade level. For example, most school districts emphasize U.S. history in Grades 5, 8, and 11. In mathematics, prealgebra is often taught in Grade 8. In science, biology is usually emphasized in Grade 10. These content decisions influence the grade placement of benchmarks.

♦ Analyze state or district tests.

You want to be sure that you and your colleagues provide the necessary instruction for any benchmark tested at a particular grade level.

♦ Consider the difficulty of each benchmark in relation to students' development.

The most difficult and complex benchmarks should be placed at the highest grade level.

+ Analyze the textbooks and other learning resources.

While most textbooks do not provide a sound basis for curriculum decisions, you should certainly consider the teaching/learning resources available to you.

+ Decide if any benchmarks require continuing development at several grade levels.

While it generally is desirable to avoid repetition from grade to grade, you and your colleagues may decide that some benchmarks should be emphasized at two or more grade levels. Here, for example, is a language arts benchmark for grades 6–8, as identified by Kendall and Marzano (1997, p. 325):

Uses paragraph form in writing.

You might decide to emphasize that benchmark in Grade 6 and reinforce it in Grades 7 and 8. In making these decisions, you should find the criteria in Figure 4.2 helpful.

The most important consideration, of course, is your knowledge of students' needs and strengths. For every benchmark, consider two questions. Could my students learn this with effective teaching? Will it really be useful to them? After you and your colleagues have tentatively identified them for your grade, check the results with the district curriculum, to be sure that there is good coordination without repetition.

REFERENCES

Gandal, M. (1995). Not all standards are created equal. *Educational Leadership*, 52 (6), 16–21.

Glatthorn, A. A. (Ed.) (1998). *Performance assessment and standards-based curricula*. Larchmont, NY: Eye on Education.

FIGURE 4.2. CRITERIA FOR EVALUATING BENCHMARKS

Are the Benchmarks...

♦ Few in number, so that students can master them?

♦ Developmentally appropriate—challenging but attainable with effort?

♦ Specified clearly?

♦ Progressive from grade to grade, building upon what has been learned before, without undue repetition?

♦ Directly related to the standards?

♦ Effectively distributed over the grades, so that one grade is not overloaded or under loaded?

♦ Current, reflecting the recommendations of experts in the field, including experienced and knowledgeable teachers?

♦ Congruent with content emphasis for that grade level?

Kendall, J. S., & Marzano, R. J. (1997). *Content knowledge: A compendium of standards and benchmarks for K-12 education.* Alexandria, VA: Association for Supervision and Curriculum Development.

Marzano, R. J., & Kendall, J. S. (1996). *A comprehensive guide to designing standards-based districts, schools, and classrooms.* Alexandria, VA: Association for Supervision and Curriculum Development.

Project 2061, American Association for the Advancement of Science. (1993). *Benchmarks for science literacy.* New York: Oxford University Press.

U. S. Department of Education. (1995). *Teachers and Goals 2000.* Washington, DC: Author.

5

DEVELOPING LONG-TERM PLANS FOR TEACHING

This chapter assumes that you have identified all the benchmarks for your grade and subject. The next step is to develop a long-term plan that is based on the way your school organizes the school year. If your school operates on a year-long schedule, then your plan should cover the entire year. However, if your school uses a semester or quarter structure with an extended period schedule, then you should develop a semester or quarter plan. This chapter explains the importance of such long-term planning and describes one process to employ in long-term planning.

UNDERSTANDING THE IMPORTANCE OF LONG-TERM PLANNING

Many teachers report that they do not make long-term plans because school life is so unpredictable. While acknowledging the legitimacy of this concern, it still makes good sense to develop such plans. They foster collaborative planning by a grade-level or subject team, because it is recommended that teachers work together in producing the plan. They provide a foundation for the more detailed unit plans, by translating the curriculum guide into a series of units. They facilitate coordination across subject lines. As explained more fully below, they provide a simple means for examining the flow of instruction in two or more related subjects. They indicate whether integration will be used as a curriculum strategy. They show the sequence of units across the year. Finally, they show clearly the time allocations teachers have made for the several units, thus facilitating communication between the teachers and the principal.

TAKING THE PRELIMINARY STEPS
FOR LONG-TERM PLANNING

You should take three preliminary steps in the planning process. The first step is to decide if you will plan alone or with colleagues. Team planning is strongly recommended because you can profit from other teachers' ideas. Team planning also ensures good coordination in the planning process, especially in relation to the use of resources.

The second step is to develop the appropriate forms. Figure 5.1 shows one form that has been used successfully with many schools; Figure 5.2 is a form that elementary teachers seem to prefer. The form in Figure 5.1 includes all the essential planning items. It first shows the weeks of the school year, in sequence. For each week it notes any events that will impact on teaching and learning, including national and state holidays, parent meetings, student extracurricular activities, and report card and parent conference days. It then notes the title of the unit, using a process explained below, and specifies the curriculum standards and related benchmarks. Some schools prefer to add a column for the textbook pages that support the unit.

FIGURE 5.1. FORM FOR YEARLY PLANNING

Team: English/social studies,   Date submitted: 9/23
        Grade 8

Weeks of Year	Important Events	Unit Title	Standard and Benchmarks
1/13–17	M. L. King birthday	Leaders who changed us	Std.: Eng. 10, Soc. Stud. 6 Bnch.: Eng 2, 4, 5, 7 Bnch.: Soc. Stud. 5, 7
1/20–24		Leaders who changed us	Std.: Eng. 10, Soc. Stud. 6 Bnch.: Eng. 1, 3 Bnch.: Soc. Stud. 2, 4
1/28–2/2	Parent night	Choosing our leaders	Std.: Eng. 10; Soc. Std. 4 Bnch.: Eng. 3, 5 Bnch.: Soc. Stud. 4

FIGURE 5.2. ALTERNATIVE FORM, ELEMENTARY

Team: 5th grade   Date submitted: 9/23

Weeks/ Subjects	1/13–17	1/20–24	1/27–31
Language Arts	Opinion letter	Letter to editor	Using computer to retrieve information
Social Studies	Great leaders	Great leaders	Choosing leaders
Science	Life in winter	Life in winter	How we stay warm
Math	Factoring	Factoring	Problem solving

The alternative form shows the four main subjects taught by elementary teachers in one column and the units indicated for each week. Although it lacks some of the details of the standard form, it does show how the several subjects relate to one another.

The third and final preliminary step is to decide when to develop the long-term plan. Some teachers develop the entire plan in the summer, modifying those decisions as they see the need. Other teams use a two-stage process. In the first stage, they develop temporary plans for the first four weeks of school, using plans that have worked before. They use those four weeks to assess student readiness, determine student needs, go over class routines, and introduce the subject. Then, with this knowledge of the students and the curriculum in mind, they move to the second stage, developing a sound plan for the rest of the year or term.

ANALYZING THE STANDARDS AND BENCHMARKS

With these preliminary steps taken, you should next analyze all the standards and benchmarks you are expected to teach during that term or year. In doing so, consider how to cluster them into one of three types of units.

♦ Standard-focused Units

These are units that focus on one standard; the standard becomes the title of the unit. Here, for example, is a U.S. history standard (as cited by Kendall & Marzano, 1997, p. 131):

Understands the causes of the Great Depression and how it affected American society.

That standard could readily be turned into a unit with this title and emphasis:

Causes and Effects of the Great Depression

The chief advantage of standard-focused units is that they are easier to plan and teach, since they deal directly with only one standard.

♦ Unified Unit

A unified unit, as the term is used here, is a unit that is based on two or more standards, from different areas of one subject or discipline. Unified curricula (such as unified science, unified math, and whole language) have been advocated by those who believe in integrating the several areas of those disciplines. Suppose, for example, that you wished to integrate U.S. history and economics, two areas within the broad field of social studies. You could develop a unit combining the standard noted above with this one from economics:

Understands basic concepts of United States fiscal policy and monetary policy. (Kendall & Marzano, 1997, p. 473)

The unit would still focus on the causes and effects of the Depression, but would give specific attention to fiscal and monetary policies as one factor.

The chief advantage of the unified unit is that it reduces the fragmentation of the curriculum and helps the students understand the relationships of the various components of a field of study. The major problem with some unified units is that they fail to deal sufficiently with the basic skills of that subject.

♦ Integrated Unit

As the term is used here, an integrated unit is one based on standards from two or more different subjects. For example, you could develop an integrated unit entitled "Living in the 1930s" that would use standards from history, economics, English language arts, and the arts.

The evidence concerning the effectiveness of curriculum integration is mixed. As pointed out by one reviewer (Vars, 1991), more than 90 studies comparing integrated and traditional curricula concluded that students learned more with the integrated approach. However, some cautions have been raised with respect to too much integration (Brophy & Alleman, 1991; Gardner & Boix-Mansilla, 1994; Roth, 1994):

- Many integrated units are poorly designed collections of activities.
- Many such units do not provide sufficient depth of subject knowledge.
- The advocates of integration seem to forget that integration is a means, not an end. (For a very helpful and balanced source for integrating the curriculum, see Jacobs, 1989.)

In addition to reflecting about the type of unit, you should also weigh several other factors affecting your decision about the focus of the units. If your state tests emphasize recall of knowledge, you should be sure that you have enough standards-focused units dealing directly with that knowledge. The organization of your textbook might also affect your decision. While you should not rely on the textbook as the basis for the curriculum, matching unit titles with text chapters simplifies the planning and teaching processes. You should also consider units that you have previously taught with good results; with some minor changes, they can be used in the new design. The primary consideration is the needs of your students. As you consider your students' abilities, knowledge, and background, you will probably conclude that they will learn more from a mix of standard-focused, unified, and integrated curricula.

The analysis of all these elements should enable you to use the standards and benchmarks to develop a tentative list of unit titles. The unit title should reflect accurately the main goal of the unit. Remember that this list is only a rough draft; you will refine and reorganize it later. Identifying tentative unit titles is similar to deciding what rooms you want in a house you are designing. Before you work out in detail how the family room will look, you get the big picture first.

Figure 5.3 is a list of unit titles developed by a team of 8th grade social studies teachers whose district guide required them to teach the nation's history from the Civil War to the present.

**FIGURE 5.3. TENTATIVE LIST OF UNIT TITLES,
GRADE 8 SOCIAL STUDIES**

Title of Unit	*Type of Unit*
1. Civil War and Reconstruction	Unified
2. The Industrial United States	Standard-focused
3. The Emergence of Modern America	Unified
4. The Great Depression	Integrated
5. World War II	Unified
6. Postwar United States	Standard-focused
7. Understanding Our Own Times	Integrated

DETERMINING THE SEQUENCE OF UNITS

Once the tentative list of titles has been developed, you should next decide on the order of units. Several sequencing principles are available. Units can be organized according to students' interests, beginning with a unit that has high interest and using seasonal progression to determine placement of other units. Second, they can be organized according to content difficulty, starting with units that would be relatively simple and then moving to more challenging ones. Third, they can be ordered chronologically, as they often are in history courses or courses emphasizing British or American literature. They can also be organized in an *expanding horizons* approach, beginning with the individual, then the family, then the community, followed by the state and the nation. Finally, they can be organized in relation to the structure of that subject, as mathematics units usually are. Obviously, you could also combine two or more of these approaches.

In addition to selecting one of these basic sequencing models, you should weigh three other factors affecting the order of units. First, such decisions may be affected by the major events taking place. For example, many elementary teachers present a unit on the Pilgrims during the Thanksgiving season. If you do so, be sure that the students have not had too many seasonal lessons. Other teachers plan a special unit on the contributions of African Americans near the Martin Luther King holiday. Second, the sequence used in other subjects should be considered. Mathematics and science should be closely correlated, as should English language arts and social studies, or language arts and visual arts.

Perhaps the most important consideration is whether the sequence adds up to a holistic conception. You should ensure that the sequence of units helps students see the big picture of that subject and make connections between units. Keep in mind a very useful recommendation made by Wolf and Reardon (1996): in planning the sequence of units, provide a developmental frame for the curriculum for both yourself and your students. A *developmental frame* is a carefully structured sequence of units that build upon each other, systematically extending the students' knowledge of that subject and its essential concepts and skills.

ALLOCATING TIME TO THE UNITS

The way you allocate time to each unit is a critical matter, because the amount of time is directly related to student learning. The time can perhaps best be represented by the number of instructional periods to be devoted to the unit; an *instructional period* is defined here as a clearly demarcated session lasting from

30 to 90 minutes. One simple process for allocating time is this one:

- Determine the total number of instructional periods available for the term or the year.

  Keep in mind the guideline that a standards-based curriculum should require no more than 80 percent of the total time available, allowing for enrichment, remediation, and the usual loss of instructional time that occurs in most schools. Thus, for example, if you are teaching a year-long course that meets every day of the school week, you should plan for approximately 130–140 periods, not 180.

- Determine the relative importance of each unit, according to district priorities and your perception of your students' needs.

- Consider the attention span of the students.

- Assess the complexity of the unit, keeping in mind the importance of depth.

- Tentatively allocate periods to each unit, based on those considerations.

- Translate the number of periods to the number of weeks required. For example, if you have allocated 15 periods and a class meets once a day, you will need 3 weeks.

TAKING THE FINAL STEPS

The next step is to record all this information in some systematic way, using whatever form you have devised. If you use a form similar to the one shown in Figure 5.1 (p. 56), you would list the weeks of the term or the year, showing the Monday to Friday dates. Then you would note any school or community events that might affect your planning and teaching, such as national holidays, parent conferences, report cards, and testing dates. Then you would note each unit title in order, using a vertical arrow to indicate a unit that occupied more than one week. Finally, to ensure that your plan deals with all the required standards and benchmarks, you should note those covered by each unit, using an easily interpreted code.

EVALUATING YOUR DECISIONS

You and your colleagues should first review your decisions, using the criteria shown in Figure 5.4. Then you should meet with your principal, to inform him or her of your decisions and to solicit constructive input.

FIGURE 5.4. CRITERIA FOR EVALUATING LONG-TERM CALENDARS

Does the long-term calendar...

♦ Reflect and correspond with the school calendar?

♦ Note significant events likely to influence teaching and learning?

♦ Organize the benchmarks into units, with titles clearly stated?

♦ Sequence the units appropriately?

♦ Allocate time appropriately?

♦ Ensure that all benchmarks are included?

♦ Reflect the importance of depth of understanding?

REFERENCES

Brophy, J., & Alleman, J. (1991). Curriculum integration isn't always a good idea. *Educational Leadership, 49* (2), 66.

Gardner, J., & Boix-Mansilla, V. (1994). Teaching for understanding in the disciplines—and beyond. *Teachers College Record, 96,* 198–218.

Jacobs, H. H. (Ed.) (1989). *Interdisciplinary curriculum: Design and implementation.* Alexandria, VA: Association for Supervision and Curriculum Development.

Kendall, J. S., & Marzano, R. J. (1997). *Content knowledge.* Alexandria, VA: Association for Supervision and Curriculum Development.

Roth, K. J. (1994). Second thoughts about interdisciplinary studies. *American Educator, 18* (1), 44–47.

Vars, G. F. (1991). Integrated curriculum in historical perspective. *Educational Leadership, 49* (2), 14–15.

Wolf, D. P., & Reardon, S. F. (1996). Can performance-based assessments contribute to the achievement of educational equity? In J. B. Baron & D. P. Wolf (Eds.), *Performance-based student assessment: Challenges and possibilities* (pp. 1–31). Chicago: University of Chicago Press.

6

DEVELOPING PERFORMANCE TASKS AND RUBRICS

Once you have developed your long-term plans for the term or year, you have two choices about the next step. You can use the long-term schedule to begin the development of units—or you can develop the performance tasks. The recommendation here is to identify the performance tasks and then shape the unit so that students can do well when the assessment is made. This chapter explains the nature of performance tasks and then presents a process for designing a performance task and its related evaluation materials.

UNDERSTANDING THE NATURE OF PERFORMANCE TASKS

A performance task is a complex open-ended problem posed for the student to solve as a means of demonstrating mastery; the performance tasks constitute the basis for the performance assessment. Marzano and Kendall (1996) identify these defining characteristics of a performance task:

- Requires knowledge to be applied to a specific situation;
- Provides necessary guidance and information to complete the task;
- Specifies learning context (independent, pairs, small groups); and
- Specifies how students will demonstrate their findings or solution.

Typically, you first develop the performance task and then use the performance task to design the unit, teach the unit, and then conduct a performance assessment to determine if the students could perform the task. Note, however, that some teachers prefer to design the unit and then the task to fit the unit.

To clarify the difference between tasks and assessments, here is an example from a fourth grade geography unit:

- The Standard

  Understands the characteristics and uses of spatial organization of Earth's surface.

- Benchmark

  Understands how changing transportation and communication technology have affected relationships between locations.

- Performance Task

  Pretend that you are a group of political leaders. You all live in Boston, Massachusetts. You often have to communicate and meet with other leaders in Washington, DC. In the first part of this task, pretend that the year is 1796. Explain in your journal how you would communicate with the Washington leaders. Then explain how you would travel from Boston to Washington. In the second part of the task, pretend that the year is 2010. Explain in your journal how you would communicate and meet with the Washington leaders.

- Performance Assessment

  The evaluators would assess the students' performance on the task.

DESIGNING THE PERFORMANCE TASK

Several steps are involved in designing a valid performance task.

DEVELOP A COMPREHENSIVE PLAN

Before you and your colleagues start developing performance tasks and assessments, you should develop a comprehensive plan that enables you to organize your work effectively. Teachers who have experience developing performance tasks and assessments have offered several suggestions about this planning process.

First, they point out that the plan should be based on the approved curriculum guide. They also suggest that the first performance task should not be presented during the first two weeks of school, because those early weeks are needed to establish routines and to get to know their students. However, some teachers report that they prefer to implement the task early in the year, because doing so gives them an opportunity to observe the students at work and learn about their learning styles and capabilities. They also recommend that the performance tasks be spaced out over the term or year, to ensure that there is ample time between tasks to assemble resources for the next task, to remediate learning, and to enrich the curriculum. If a given classroom performance task is to be used to prepare for state performance assessments, then it should be implemented just prior to the state test. Be sure, of course, that you act ethically in such preparation. Finally, they strongly recommend that developers should take their time in developing the tasks and making the assessments, building in quality control checks along the way.

One useful approach to planning is to develop a detailed planning schedule for the first performance task similar to the one shown in Figure 6.1 (p. 70). Implement that schedule flexibly. Then, on the basis of what you have learned from that first task, prepare a comprehensive plan for developing and testing the rest of the performance tasks. If you and your colleagues have successfully developed the first performance task together, you may decide to work on your own in developing the next batch. The schedule shown in the table could be accelerated, of course, by giving the team special release time during the school year or by paying them to work during the summer.

FIGURE 6.1. SCHEDULE FOR DEVELOPING
ONE PERFORMANCE TASK

Step	Target Date
1. Review standards, benchmarks, unit titles	June 1
2. Develop draft of task	July 1
3. Do self-evaluation of draft.	July 8
4. Secure review by colleagues	July 15
5. Secure external review	July 22
6. Revise draft	July 29
7. Develop criteria and rubrics	August 15
8. Have criteria and rubrics reviewed by colleagues and external reviewers	August 29
9. Field test all materials	October 10
10. Evaluate results of field test	November 1
11. Revise and disseminate to teachers	December 15

REVIEW STANDARDS, BENCHMARKS, AND UNIT TITLES

With this preliminary planning accomplished, you and your team should be ready to develop the first performance task. Obviously there is no right way to do this. The process explained below draws from the extensive literature in the field and the recommendations of teachers who have developed valid tasks. Note that the process should be implemented flexibly. The discussion that follows explains how a fifth-grade team developed a performance task for social studies, using the following Grade 5 social studies standard and benchmarks (drawn and paraphrased from the Kendall & Marzano, 1997, compilation).

- ♦ Standard: Understands institutions of government created during the Revolution.

♦ Benchmarks:

- Understands major political issues in the 13 colonies.

- Understands controversies at the Constitutional Convention.

- Understands differences in leaders, especially Hamilton and Jefferson.

REVIEW YOUR EARLIER DECISION ABOUT THE UNIT TITLE AND THE TIME ALLOCATION

Since initially identifying the title and the time, you may have reconsidered your initial choices. The team working on the standards and benchmarks noted above have decided to call the unit "Fighting It Out at the Constitutional Convention." They now believe they will need three weeks for the unit.

REFLECT ABOUT THE STUDENTS—THEIR INTERESTS, THEIR KNOWLEDGE, THEIR NEEDS

The team members realize that their fifth graders probably have no knowledge at all of the forming of the Constitution and are unlikely to be strongly interested in the topic. However, they also believe that this period is a crucial one in the formation of the nation's governmental system. They think that they can stimulate interest by referring to the ongoing controversy over federal powers and states' rights.

REFLECT ABOUT THE STANDARD AND THE BENCHMARKS

While reflecting about the standard and the benchmarks, also consider the related classroom learning objectives. If the objectives have not been identified previously, the team should do so at this time. For example, the first benchmark in the above example might be analyzed into these learning objectives.

♦ Identifies abolition as key issue.

♦ Identifies federal and state powers as key issue.

♦ Identifies separation of powers as key issue.

REFLECT ABOUT THE WAYS THAT STUDENTS MIGHT DEMONSTRATE THEIR LEARNING IN THE PERFORMANCE ASSESSMENT

Thinking about the types of performance assessments may stimulate some specific ideas. McTighe and Ferrara (1997) present a very useful typology of performance assessments (paraphrased as follows).

- *Constructed Responses:* Short answer; diagrams; visuals (such as a concept map).

- *Products:* Essay; research paper and laboratory report; log or journal; story, play, or poem; portfolio; art or science exhibit; model; video- or audiotape; spreadsheet.

- *Performances:* Oral report; dance; science demonstration; athletic competition; dramatic reading; enactment; debate; recital.

- *Processes:* Oral questioning; observation; interview; conference; process description; learning log; record of thinking processes.

CONSIDER THE PURPOSES OF THE ASSESSMENT

McTighe and Ferrara (1997) suggest these multiple purposes: diagnosis of student strengths and problems; feedback on learning; guidance of instruction; motivation of performance; practice; evaluation or grading; program evaluation. Stiggins (1997) stresses that well-designed performance assessments are a highly effective teaching tool, significantly fostering student learning.

BRAINSTORM THE PERFORMANCE TASKS THAT MIGHT BE USED

Suspending critical judgment, team members should do some freewheeling creative thinking, simply listing all the possibilities. Here are some of the ideas that the fifth-grade team put on the table:

+ Give a speech on either side of one of the issues.
+ Publish a newspaper that might have appeared at the time.
+ Role play Thomas Jefferson or Alexander Hamilton.
+ Make a "You Are There" videotape.
+ Write a diary of a representative to the Continental Congress.
+ Stage a session of the Continental Congress.
+ Write a critique of the Articles of Confederation.

PRELIMINARILY EVALUATE THE BRAINSTORMING RESULTS

Make a preliminary evaluation of the brainstorming results, and combine ideas or select the one that seems most promising. At this stage, the team should assess the results of the brainstorming. The assessment here should involve two components: a validity check and a reality check.

The validity check answers the central question: "Will this performance task enable students to acquire and use the skills and knowledge embodied in the standards and benchmarks?" If a performance task seems stimulating and motivating but does not relate directly to the standards and benchmarks, then it is seriously flawed.

The reality check answers this question: "Will it work in the classroom?" In making the reality check, you should examine such issues as student interest in the task, the knowledge resources required, the time the task will take, and the teachability of the task. A more systematic evaluation of the performance task will take place later, as explained below.

Here is the first draft of a performance task that might result from reviewing the brainstorming results in the example.

Pretend that you are a representative from one of the 13 colonies to the Continental Congress. Present a speech expressing your views on one of the issues and controversies facing that group.

DEVELOP A SCENARIO FOR THE PERFORMANCE TASK AND THE INSTRUCTION REQUIRED

A scenario is a mental picture of how the classroom events unroll—how the class is organized, how the unit starts, how it progresses, and how it ends. The scenario need not be committed to paper; it is simply a planning tool that gives you a clearer picture of how the task and the teaching work together. Here is the scenario that might be developed for the task listed above:

> Organize the class into groups of three each—one student per issue. Use the *jigsaw* cooperative learning process to make each student an expert on his or her issue. Each expert returns to his or her group and teaches the others. Each group chooses one of the 13 states that it will represent. The expert from each group makes a speech about the issue he or she knows best. The others in the group help prepare the speech.

Note that the scenario yields a general picture. It is a visioning process that helps you further test the teachability of the task and its accompanying instruction.

EVALUATE THE FIRST DRAFT OF THE PERFORMANCE TASK AND REVISE ACCORDINGLY

At this stage a more systematic evaluation by the team is useful. The criteria listed in Figure 6.2 are helpful in the evaluation process. (The following sources were useful in deriving the criteria: Herman, Aschbacher, & Winters, 1992; Wiggins, 1996.)

In the example used above, this initial evaluation would indicate to the developers at least one major deficiency: the performance task as stated did not adequately assess the students' mastery of the benchmark relating to Hamilton and Jefferson. The task would therefore be revised, with this addition to the original:

> Each individual is also required to write a letter to a friend at home. The letter should report on the progress being made in the Continental Congress, specifically contrasting the leadership of Hamilton and Jefferson.

FIGURE 6.2. CRITERIA FOR EVALUATING
PERFORMANCE TASKS

Does the performance task...

- Correspond closely and comprehensively with the standard and benchmarks it is designed to assess?

- Require the students to access prior knowledge, acquire new knowledge, and use that knowledge in completing the task?

- Require the use of higher thought processes, including creative thinking?

- Seem real and purposeful, embedded in a meaningful context that seems authentic?

- Engage the students' interest?

- Require the students to communicate to classmates and others the processes they used and the results they obtained, using multiple response modes?

- Require sustained effort over a significant period of time?

- Provide the student with options?

- Seem feasible in the context of schools and classrooms, not requiring inordinate resources or creating undue controversy?

- Convey a sense of fairness to all, being free of bias?

- Challenge the students?

- Include criteria and rubrics for evaluating student performance?

- Provide for both group and individual work, with appropriate accountability?

REVIEW STANDARDS, BENCHMARKS, AND UNIT TITLES: ANOTHER EXAMPLE

Here is another example showing how a team developed a performance task from standards and benchmarks. After reviewing the standards for English language arts, a seventh grade language arts/social studies team decided to develop a unified task for these standards (paraphrased from Kendall & Marzano, 1997.)

- ◆ Demonstrates competence in the general skills of the writing process.
- ◆ Gathers and uses information for research purposes.
- ◆ Demonstrates competence in the skills for reading informational texts.
- ◆ Demonstrates competence in speaking and listening.

They had previously identified the unit title as "Researching to Inform." After reflecting about each standard, they identified these benchmarks from among those that had been assigned to seventh grade.

- ◆ Demonstrates competence in the general skills of the writing process.
  - • Writes expository texts, using the writing process flexibly.
  - • Uses the conventions of written English correctly: correct word choice, sentence structure, usage, punctuation, capitalization.
- ◆ Gathers and uses information for research purposes.
  - • Gathers data from interviews.
  - • Uses computer sources.
  - • Determines the appropriateness of information sources.

♦ Demonstrates competence in the skills for reading informational texts.

- Applies reading skills to a variety of informational texts.
- Summarizes and paraphrases complex structures from informational texts.
- Differentiates between fact and opinion in informational texts.

♦ Demonstrates competence in speaking and listening.

- Plays a variety of roles in group discussions.

Here is the draft of the performance task they developed after working through the process explained above.

The school's guidance counselor has informed you that there is a need for guidance materials at the 4th–5th grade levels. These topics have been identified as those for which materials are most needed:

- When your parents divorce.
- Living in harmony with brothers and sisters.
- Keeping physically fit.
- Coping with negative feelings.

Your group will be assigned one of these topics. Your first job is to find current and reliable sources of information about your topic. You are then expected to summarize what you have learned. Finally, you are to present the information in a form that will both interest and inform your audience of 4th and 5th graders. Both your teacher and the students for whom you are writing will judge the effectiveness of your materials.

In addition to contributing to the group's performance, you are required to write a brief in-class report (without notes) on these three topics: conducting interviews; writing a summary; and evaluating information sources.

As you and your colleagues review this performance task, you should reflect about how you might improve it.

EVALUATE THE PERFORMANCE TASK

As you will note in Figure 6.1 (p. 70), four types of evaluation are recommended: self-evaluation by the team; review by colleagues; evaluation by external reviewer; and a field test. While this may seem to represent too much evaluation, keep in mind that your materials will be used by other teachers in subsequent years. A comprehensive evaluation is required if your work is to be of high quality. The first three evaluations (self, colleagues, external reviewer) can be based on the criteria shown in Figure 6.2 (p. 75). In assessing the results of the field test, you and your colleagues should base your judgments on three data sources: students' performance on the field test assessment; student survey; and teacher interview. Some teachers report that they find it helpful to develop rubrics that will assist in evaluating the materials.

DEVELOPING CRITERIA AND RUBRICS FOR EVALUATING STUDENT PERFORMANCE

Once you have the performance task in good shape, you should next develop criteria and rubrics to assist in the assessment process. To accomplish this goal, you need to understand how some key terms are being used. (The discussion that follows draws from these sources: Goodrich, 1996; Herman, Aschbacher, & Winters, 1992; and Marzano, Pickering, & McTighe, 1993.)

Criteria are the components of quality that are used as the basis for evaluation. Thus, if you were evaluating a football quarterback, you might use these criteria: passing completion; play-calling ability; avoidance of interceptions; running ability. A *performance standard* is a statement of expected quality of the performance. Thus, a football coach might set this standard for passing accuracy in choosing quarterbacks: "We expect at least a 50% completion rate before we consider any other factors." A *rubric* is a scoring or evaluation tool that lists each criterion and indicates several levels of performance. Figure 6.3 shows part of the rubric that would be used in assessing the students' performance on the speech to the Continental Congress. These rubrics would be used to evaluate each student presenting a speech; separate rubrics would be developed for the individual letters.

FIGURE 6.3. RUBRIC FOR SCORING SPEECHES

Criteria/ Levels	Unsatis- factory	Minimally Satisfac- tory	More Than Sat- isfactory	Very Good	Superior
Group Work	Does not contrib- ute to group; of- ten dis- rupts	Makes a few contri butions; disrupts occasion- ally	Makes several contribu- tions, with no disrup- tions	Makes several useful contribu- tions; fa- cilitates group work	Makes several valuable contribu- tions; provides leader- ship
Use of Histori- cal Knowl- edge					
Rea- soning Ability					
Commu- nication Skill					
Other					

There are several reasons why you should develop and use criteria and rubrics. First, they facilitate quality performance by making clear to the student what is expected. In too many classrooms, students are "flying blind," with no clear knowledge of what constitutes satisfactory performance. In such classrooms, teacher feedback is minimal and unclear and uses such value language as "try harder," "not your best effort," "not up to my standards." One teacher reports that she staples a copy of the rubrics to the student's paper, grading the student specifically on rubrics.

The criteria and rubrics are also useful to the teacher in three ways. First, they provide helpful guidance in preparing and instructing the students. If you have a clear idea of the criteria, you can give the students the specific help they need to embody those elements in their performance. Second, they also help the teacher by facilitating the evaluation process, making it more fair, consistent, and valid. You can do a better job of grading students if you know the rubrics. Finally, they help parents understand more clearly what students are being evaluated for and how grades are assigned.

The first step in developing rubrics is to identify the criteria you will use. Practice has shown that four to seven criteria seem to work best. If there are too few, the feedback is not specific enough. If there are too many, the evaluation process becomes too complicated. You derive the criteria by answering these related questions: "What factors contribute to the overall performance? What do I look for when I evaluate this performance? What elements will make a difference in the quality?"

Suppose, for example, that a fifth grade teacher living in a coastal community has taught a unit on ocean pollution. She has designed a performance task that requires the students to develop for their community a practical plan for reducing ocean pollution; they also must sell their plan to their community leaders. She thinks about the plan she might develop and the means by which she would convince community leaders. What criteria would she use to judge her plan? She might identify these:

♦ Scientific soundness
♦ Political astuteness
♦ Quality of the writing

She then reflects about how she might modify those criteria for her students, so that they are developmentally appropriate. She decides to change "political astuteness" to "knowledge of elected officials."

Here is another example. One of the standards for health as a subject is this one: "Knows how to maintain mental and emotional health" (Kendall & Marzano, 1997, p. 544). This is the benchmark for which a fourth grade teacher wants to develop a performance task: "Knows common sources of stress for children and ways to manage stress." The teacher develops this performance task:

> Each group will make a presentation to one of our 3rd grade classes. The presentation will be on this topic: "How to manage stress." You must develop visual materials that will interest 3rd graders. Your presentation will help the students understand what stress is, what causes it for children, and how children can best handle it.

What criteria would you use to evaluate the presentations? Here are some that come to mind:

◆ Accuracy of content

◆ Appropriateness of vocabulary

◆ Effectiveness of visual aids

◆ Effectiveness of relationships with audience

Once you have established the criteria to be used in developing the rubrics, you then decide how many levels of performance you will describe for each criterion. A review of the examples provided in the literature indicates that a range of three to six levels is common. Some teachers recommend that you identify the number of levels that corresponds with the number of report card grades. Thus, if your school uses the standard A/B/C/D/F system, it is easier for you and the students if you use five levels. Several experts recommend that you use an even number of levels, thus curbing the tendency of teachers to assign a middle score.

One concern about having several levels is that the more levels of performance that you specify, the more difficult is the task of writing rubrics. For that reason, you may wish to begin with three levels of performance and then move to five when you and your students become more accustomed to using rubrics.

After deciding on the criteria and the number of levels, you then specify the two extremes—best and worst. Suppose, for example, that one of your criteria for a task of writing a persuasive letter to the editor is "writing effectiveness." You would ask yourself, "What would an A letter look like? What distinguishing features would it have?" Here are some that you might identify:

> Uses correct business letter form, uses language appropriate to audience, is clearly organized, is free of mechanical errors.

You then ask yourself, "What would an F letter look like?" These characteristics seem important:

> Has several errors in form, makes inappropriate word choice, is confusing in organization, makes several mechanical errors.

Then you fill in the midpoints. For example, these might be the characteristics of a C paper:

> Makes 3–4 errors in form, makes 2–3 errors in word choice, uses clear organization without signaling, makes 2–3 mechanical errors.

In the same way, you would analyze the remaining levels of performance for that criterion. (See Goodrich, 1996, for another perspective on writing rubrics.)

Here is another example, based on the performance task for fourth graders that requires them to make a presentation to third graders on managing stress. The discussion will take you through the process of writing rubrics.

- ◆ Identify criteria

    These were previously identified: accuracy of content; appropriateness of vocabulary; effectiveness of visual aids; effectiveness of relationship with audience.

- ◆ Specify number of levels of performance

    In this case, three levels are used: "more than satisfactory"; "satisfactory"; and "less than satisfactory."

- Take the first criterion and indicate the features of the best response

  This is the primary feature of a "more than satisfactory" response on the criterion "accuracy of content": "presents content that is accurate in all respects."

- For that same criterion, indicate the features of a "less than satisfactory" response

  "Presents content that is inaccurate in several important respects."

- For that same criterion, indicate the features of a "satisfactory" response

  "Makes one or two minor errors in content."

Then you would proceed to the next criterion and repeat the process until all criterion are defined.

USING A STANDARD FORMAT TO SYSTEMATIZE THE PRODUCTS

With the performance task, the criteria, and the rubrics developed, the next step is to systematize all these decisions using a standard format. First, provide the necessary identifying information: school district; school; developers; subject; grade level; title; recommended time allocation. Then clearly specify three basic elements: the context; the task; the rubrics. The context identifies the setting—the time and the place—and the student's role. Here is how the context for the Constitutional Convention task might be presented.

> The year is 1787. The place is Philadelphia. You are a representative from 1 of the 13 original states. You are part of a team representing your state at the Constitutional Convention. The convention is working to establish the basis for the government of the new nation. Three issues divide the members. Should slavery be outlawed? Should the states or the federal government have more power? How should we sep-

arate the power of the President and the power of the Congress?

Then the task is presented, with clear and specific detail. The students must have a very clear understanding of the problem they are to solve or of the performance they are to present. Here is how the task might be specified in the above example:

> You will become an expert on one of these issues. With the help of your team, you will prepare and deliver a speech about that issue to the Convention. Your speech should make clear your team's opinion about the issue. Your speech should last between 5 and 10 minutes. You want to persuade the rest of the Convention members to believe as you do.

You then include the rubrics that have been developed. You also include any individual tasks that you have included to assess each student's mastery. In the example used above, the team would include the individual task of writing a letter about Hamilton and Jefferson.

Remember the importance of evaluation. You and your team should first evaluate your own work. Then have other colleagues check it. Secure input from an external reviewer. And field test all materials.

Finally, be sure to develop your own archive of student work. It is helpful to collect what are called "anchor papers," papers that clearly represent an exemplary response for each level. Thus, you can say to a student, "This is what an A paper would read like." Other examples should also be preserved for demonstrating the nature of excellence, such as videotapes of speeches.

REFERENCES

Goodrich, H. (1996). Understanding rubrics. *Educational Leadership, 54* (4), 14–17.

Herman, J. L., Aschbacher, P. R., & Winters, L. (1992). *A practical guide to alternative assessment.* Alexandria, VA: Association for Supervision and Curriculum Development.

Kendall, J. S., & Marzano, R. J. (1997). *Content knowledge.* Aurora, CO: Mid-Continent Regional Educational Laboratory.

Marzano, R. J., & Kendall, J. S. (1996). *A comprehensive guide to designing standards-based districts, schools, and classrooms.* Alexandria, VA: Association for Supervision and Curriculum Development.

Marzano, R. J., Pickering, D., & McTighe, J. (1993). *Assessing student outcomes.* Alexandria, VA: Association for Supervision and Curriculum Development.

McTighe, J., & Ferrara, S. (1997). *Assessing learning in the classroom.* Washington, DC: National Education Association.

Stiggins, R. J. (1997). *Student-centered classroom assessment* (2nd ed.). Columbus, OH: Merrill.

Wiggins, G. (1996). Practicing what we preach in designing authentic assessments? *Educational Leadership, 54* (4), 18–25.

7

DEVELOPING UNITS BASED ON PERFORMANCE TASKS

Some teachers move from the design of the performance task to its implementation, without bothering to develop a unit. In their view, the task is the unit. However, you may wish to consider the desirability of designing a unit around the task. Doing so makes it easier for you and other teachers to organize learning in a comprehensive and systematic way. Read this chapter carefully and then make up your mind about unit development.

UNDERSTAND THE IMPORTANCE OF UNIT PLANNING

Planning units based on performance tasks helps you plan and facilitate student achievement. Several arguments can be advanced for developing units, rather than simply presenting the task to students and focusing on single lessons. The unit emphasizes unified and cohesive elements of the curriculum, not fragmented pieces. The unit is broad enough to encompass systematically the skills needed for the performance assessment. The unit shows the students the relationship of parts. The unit is the best structure for organizing problem-solving activities. And the unit provides a solid base for your own teaching.

ANALYZE THE PERFORMANCE TASK

The first step in the process of developing assessment-based units is to analyze the performance task, keeping in mind the nature of authentic learning. An example from Grade 6 science illustrates the ways in which such an analysis of the performance task can be made. Assume that this is the standard:

Understand energy sources and their relationship to heat and temperature (paraphrased from Kendall & Marzano, 1997).

These are the Grade 6 benchmarks that are derived from that standard:

- Knows that heat is a form of energy.
- Defines *heat* and *temperature*, clarifying the distinction.
- Explains the relationship of heat and mass.
- Explains how heat moves: conduction, convection, radiation.
- Knows the sources of heat.
- Knows how heat can be conserved, including using insulation.

From that standard and those benchmarks, a team of science teachers had tentatively identified the unit title as, "You're Getting Warm—Understanding Heat." Using the processes explained in the previous chapter, they then developed this performance task (an abbreviated version is presented here, as an example):

- Group Task

  You and your group have been asked to make a presentation to 5th graders on a practical application of information about heat. The presentation will last 15 minutes and will include the use of visuals. Each group will be assigned one of these topics:

  - Keeping warm in an emergency
  - Saving heating costs in your home.
  - Saving heating costs in our school.
  - Preserving resources.

  Arrangements will be made to present your report to one of our 5th grade classes. A high school science teacher will judge the accuracy of your information. The 5th-grade class will judge the effectiveness of your presentation.

♦ Individual Task

Keep a science journal in which you record how your understanding of heat changes throughout the course of this unit, including the results of your own scientific experimentation.

As explained earlier, you should develop a unit scenario as a way of testing the feasibility and likely effectiveness of the performance task and the instruction required. The unit scenario is a mental picture of how the unit begins, unfolds, and ends. It is a kind of mental experiment, to see how your plans might work in practice. You reflect about several issues: your students; the standard and its related benchmarks; the performance task; the nature of authentic learning and teaching; the resources available; and the time available. This is a scenario for the heat task:

Begin the unit by talking about the coming winter. Ask the students to write what they know about heat. Give an overview of the unit, focusing on the performance task. Have the students view a video on heat, followed by some simple experiments on heat movement. Teach them interviewing skills, so that they can get good current information about their topic. Organize the groups. Monitor their work as it progresses. Check first drafts and arrange for high school teacher review. Work out details of presentation to fifth graders. Debrief the whole unit.

This scenario is only a general and tentative picture of how the unit might unfold. Other scenarios are possible, of course.

With the scenario in mind, the next step in translating the performance task into a unit is to determine what knowledge students will need to complete the task successfully. Research has demonstrated conclusively that expert problem-solvers operate from a deep knowledge of the subject (see, for example, Leithwood & Steinbach, 1995).You determine what knowledge students will need by reviewing the standards and benchmarks and by analyzing the knowledge demands of the task. In carrying out this critical analysis, make a comprehensive list and then review it, keeping in mind the cognitive development of the learners.

Here are the results of this review and analysis of the heat task:

♦ Knows that heat is a form of energy.

♦ Distinguishes between *heat* and *temperature*.

♦ Knows the relationship between heat and mass.

♦ Knows how heat moves.

♦ Knows heat sources.

♦ Knows how to conserve heat.

♦ Knows how to apply knowledge in practical situations.

Once you have identified the knowledge needed, you next decide how students will gain access to or acquire that knowledge. Here are some options to consider: listen to teacher or guest presenter; view a video; use a computer; learn from trained peers; read text and other print materials; listen to audio cassettes; interview expert; conduct an experiment. The simplest and most direct means of facilitating access is for you to present the knowledge. Even though teacher lecture has been ridiculed as hopelessly old-fashioned, it still can be an effective tool in the hands of an expert teacher. Keep in mind, however, that not all students can learn by listening. Also, varying the means of access will probably enhance student interest.

The next step is to analyze the *learning strategies* that students need to master to complete the task successfully. As the term is used here, a *learning strategy* is a complex mental operation used in solving a problem. In previous years, they were called *thinking skills*. Some strategies are subject specific, such as this one for mathematics: in solving a math problem, identify the knowns. Some can be used in several subjects, such as this one: organize information by using a matrix. Again, make a comprehensive list, such as this one for the heat task.

♦ Evaluating sources of knowledge

♦ Organizing and storing knowledge

- Devising and implementing a scientific experiment to gather evidence
- Interviewing
- Making a presentation with visuals
- Adapting to audience

After reflecting about the time available, what the students already know, and what is absolutely essential for them to know, identify one or two strategies to teach in the unit. Experts now agree that such strategies are best taught in the context of real problems to solve, not as isolated skills. For example, in the list above, the team might decide to teach only two: interviewing and making a presentation with visuals.

Next you should determine the specific steps that students should take in completing the performance task, once they have acquired the necessary knowledge and can use the strategy. You do this through a *task analysis*, asking yourself this question: "If I were a fifth grader, what steps would I take in completing the task?" Here is a list for the heat task:

- Interview expert
- Carry out experiments
- Synthesize information into initial list
- Write text for presentation
- Add visuals
- Check for scientific accuracy
- Practice presentation, with feedback

At this stage you should also firm up your decisions about the classroom learning objectives by reviewing all the decisions you have made thus far. It is also a good time to identify the learning resources your students will need.

Finally, you and your team members need to determine both the formative and the summative assessments that you will make. The *formative assessments* are those you make during the learning process. Here are some of the ways you can make formative assessments: evaluate work samples in progress; observe students at work; administer a written quiz; evaluate homework; conduct a recitation; have students write in journals. The *summative assessment* is the performance assessment, when you and the other assessors make a final judgment about student performance.

All these decisions can be recorded on a form similar to that shown in Figure 7.1. Most teachers who have used it report that they have found it to be useful. Down the left side are listed the standard components of an assessment-based unit: knowledge acquisition; learning strategy; performance task steps; classroom learning objectives; resources; and assessment. Across the top are listed the days of the unit—a two-week unit would have 10 days; a three-week unit, 15 days. In Figure 7.1, to conserve space, only the first three days are shown.

A form such as that in Figure 7.1 serves several important functions. It reminds you and your team of the major components you should include. By examining the form with a horizontal perspective, you can see how the individual lessons build upon each other and how knowledge and strategies are developed. By examining the form with a vertical perspective, you can check the content of the lesson plan for a given day.

PREPARE THE UNIT FOR EVALUATION

Now that you have a general sense of how the unit develops into lessons, you should package the unit for teacher evaluation and use. At this stage, keep in mind especially the needs of the teachers who will be using it. You want them to have some flexibility in teaching the unit, while at the same time providing sufficient guidance. Here are the components that are usually included in assessment-driven units, in the order in which they are usually presented:

- ♦ Identifying information: school district and address, names of developers, date of publication
- ♦ Title of the unit.
- ♦ School subject and grade level of intended use.
- ♦ Suggested number of lessons.
- ♦ Curriculum standard and benchmarks addressed.
- ♦ Classroom learning objectives.

FIGURE 7.1. UNIT PLANNING FORM

Component	Day 1	Day 2	Day 3
Acquire Knowledge	Activate prior knowledge; View video on heat	Experiment: heat movement	
Acquire Strategies			Interviewing
Complete Task			
Classroom Learning Objectives	Heat, energy; heat, temperature; heat, mass; heat sources	Conduction; convection radiation	
Resources	Video, "The Power of Heat"		
Assess Learning	Assess prior knowledge		
Other	Establish need; provide overview		

- Performance task with criteria and rubrics.
- Form for evaluating the unit.

Instead of writing out all this information, you may include only the identifying information and the chart.

ARRANGE FOR EVALUATION OF THE UNIT

Each unit should undergo several types of evaluation, using either the criteria shown in Figure 7.2 or your own set of criteria. First, as you develop and then complete the unit, you and your colleagues should do a formative evaluation, checking periodically to ensure that you are developing quality materials. When you have finished preparing the unit, you should then do a summative evaluation using the same criteria. After making any needed revisions, you should ask teachers who will be using the unit to review and evaluate it, using the criteria and giving you specific suggestions for improving it. You should embody their suggestions in another revision. The real test comes when the students use it. Here the most important criterion is the unit's effectiveness in preparing students to master the performance task. Teachers should supply written feedback on how well the students performed on the task specified.

FIGURE 7.2. CRITERIA FOR EVALUATING UNITS

Does the unit…

- Prepare the students to achieve mastery of the performance task?
- Embody the elements of authentic learning?
- Use a realistic time frame?
- Facilitate teacher use in format, organization, and content?
- Include all the components specified by the district curriculum office?
- Use language effectively and correctly?

REFERENCES

Kendall, J. S., & Marzano, R. J. (1997). *Content knowledge.* Aurora, CO: Mid-Continent Regional Educational Laboratory.

Leithwood, K., & Steinbach, R. (1995). *Expert problem solving.* Albany, NY: State University of New York Press.

Part III

TEACHING FOR SUCCESS

8

IMPLEMENTING UNITS: USING ASSESSMENT-DRIVEN INSTRUCTION

By this time you have developed a performance task. You may or may not have made a unit plan with the performance task at the center. In either case, you should be ready to use the performance task as the basis of your teaching. This chapter explains one model of teaching that has assessment at its center and then offers some suggestions about using the model effectively. Because you should not find the model very different from the way you have been teaching, you should need to make only minor adjustments in your accustomed methods.

UNDERSTANDING
ASSESSMENT-DRIVEN INSTRUCTION

In deciding how to implement the task and the unit, consider using assessment-driven instruction, a model of teaching that focuses on the performance task and its assessment. *Assessment-driven instruction* (ADI) is teaching and planning for teaching that are based upon, derive from, and focus on the performance task and its performance assessment. ADI coaches students to help them accomplish the performance task and prepare them for the performance assessment. To understand the special nature of ADI, consider the three basic elements of classroom life: curriculum, instruction, and assessment. Both ADI and the standard approach begin with the curriculum, as you decide what to teach. In the standard approach, you next instruct students and then assess their performance. In the ADI model, the performance task is designed—and then teachers instruct accordingly, coaching students to perform well on the performance assessment.

TEACHING TO THE TEST AND ADI

Many teachers *teach to the test,* preparing students to take such high-stake examinations as standardized tests, state accountability tests, district-developed graduation tests, and teacher-made tests. (See, for example, Herman & Golan, 1991.) While ADI may seem like teaching to the test, there are some key differences. To understand those differences consider these two classroom illustrations:

♦ Teaching to the Test

Students have to take a short-answer objective test that assesses their knowledge of the legislative process as employed in their state; for example, the students will be asked to define *bill* and *law.* The specific content of the test is confidential, with the test administered under conditions of high security. The teacher has identified the questions the test is likely to ask by reviewing previous editions of the test. The teacher prepares practice material on testlike items. Students spend most of their class time completing the practice exercises and checking their answers.

♦ Assessment-Driven Instruction

The teacher has developed a performance task and assessment: students will develop an action plan designed to persuade the state legislature to enact legislation for solving a community problem the students have identified. The students' action plans will be presented to the state legislator representing their district, who has agreed to judge the plans on the basis of their likely effectiveness. The teacher has explained the performance task and assessment to the students and has provided them with the criteria the legislator will use in assessing their action plan. The class is organized into four groups, each of which will identify a problem and develop its own action plan. The teacher helps the groups use class time to analyze the problem, understand the legislative process as it really works, and develop a feasible and realistic plan.

Notice that the fundamental difference involves the nature of the assessment. If the assessment is concerned only with knowledge, the teacher figures out which terms will be tested, uses direct instruction and drill-and-practice to teach the terms, helps students memorize definitions, and checks their learning with practice tests. Such teaching to the test, when accompanied by an emphasis on teacher accountability has several negative consequences. The curriculum is narrowed to what is likely to appear on the test; learning is fragmented, with students concentrating on bits and pieces of knowledge isolated from a real context; teaching is didactic; and the learning process bores the students. (For a detailed picture of such classrooms, see McNeil, 1986.) Also, many would consider such test preparation as professionally unethical. (See, for example, Mehrens & Kaminski, 1989.)

On the other hand, if an authentic performance task and assessment have been developed, then more exciting teaching and learning are likely to occur. In the example given, if the teacher and the students know that a feasible and effective action plan is to be presented, then the teacher would plan for learning activities that help students make the necessary preparations—identifying the problem, searching the knowledge base, interviewing legislators, developing a schedule, and evaluating the details of the plan.

Several studies conclude that the use of performance tasks and assessments has many positive effects: students acquire in-depth knowledge; students demonstrate more interest in and more positive attitudes toward learning; students use higher thought processes; and students perform well on traditional tests. (See Gooding, 1994; Newmann, Secada, & Wehlage, 1995; Kattri, Kane, & Reeve, 1995; and Mayer, 1998.) Also, preparing students for performance assessments is clearly ethical, because the nature of the performance assessment is a matter of public knowledge, and the evaluators assume that the students have been adequately prepared.

RATIONALE FOR USING ADI

If you decide to use the ADI model, you should be able to present a convincing rationale to other teachers, to parents, and to students. If the performance assessment is a valid measure of the mastery of complex skills and knowledge, and if ADI has been implemented effectively, then these assumptions would prevail:

♦ ADI is more likely to enable students to perform better on real-life learning tasks.

   While no one can ever guarantee learner outcomes, the research in general indicates that effective instruction achieves its intended outcomes. (See, for example, Walberg, 1995.) Thus, there is greater likelihood of transfer of learning, because the assessment should be based on a real-life context.

♦ ADI is more likely to result in quality teaching.

   Rather than fostering the continued use of drill books and practice exercises, ADI helps teachers plan for learning that involves students in meaningful and purposeful problem-solving activities. Effectively applied, ADI meets the three criteria for what Newmann, Marks, and Gamoran (1995) call "authentic pedagogy": it requires students to produce knowledge and apply it in creating products; it emphasizes disciplined inquiry; and it has value beyond school.

♦ ADI is more likely to result in more effective schools.

   If applied effectively across the school, ADI strengthens and brings into congruence several of the key elements of effective schools: a coordinated curriculum; effective teaching; and authentic assessment. (See Cotton, 1995.)

Delineating these advantages is not to suggest that ADI is without its challenges. It requires greater skill on the part of teachers. Developing valid performance assessments is a complex skill, one that teachers can acquire only with a great deal of assistance and support. It asks the principal to develop a new approach to staff development and teacher supervision—one that provides the needed coaching and feedback. And it requires students to perform in new and challenging ways. They have to think critically, solve complex problems, and communicate their results.

SUGGESTIONS FOR USING ADI

While there is no intent here to prescribe the *right* way to teach, the following suggestions are helpful in preparing students for the performance task and assessment. The suggestions are divided into two groups: the major steps taken in sequence and the processes used on a continuing basis. As you consider these steps, consider how you might adapt them to fit your own teaching style.

COMPLETE THE MAJOR STEPS IN SEQUENCE

These are the major steps you ordinarily would take in the sequence shown.

ORGANIZE

The first step is to organize the class in relation to the group structure for accomplishing the performance task. There are three choices: You can use a whole-class organization, in which the entire class works together as a unit in completing the performance task. You can use an individualized structure, in which all students work independently. Or you can use a group structure, in which small groups of students work together. For most classes, a group structure should work best (Slavin, 1990). However, if you use a group structure, remember that for maximum effectiveness, you should have a system that keeps both the group and the individual members mutually accountable. You also should ensure that all members have a clear understanding of group goals.

ENGAGE

The next step is to engage students' interest by helping them make connections with the performance task. Here are several rationales for the performance task that can facilitate student engagement:

- The task is inherently interesting and mind-stretching.
- The task will help you learn key concepts and skills in this subject.
- The task will help you apply your knowledge in solving an important problem.
- The task is similar to those you will confront in the future.
- Completing the task will enable you to share your knowledge with your classmates and learn from them.

Here is an example of how you might help students make connections.

> Most of you have a pet that spends time outside. We're going to design a pet enclosure that uses the least amount of fencing. In the process of doing this, you'll also learn some important geometry concepts.

ACTIVATE

The next step is to help students activate their prior knowledge about the task and its related components. Doing so helps you determine how much mislearning has to be corrected. It also helps you decide how much new knowledge students need to accomplish the task. You can help them activate knowledge in several ways:

- Have students work in pairs, with each member taking turns telling what he or she knows. The teacher resolves differences.
- Ask students to represent their knowledge by drawing a picture or a schematic showing how they conceptualize it.
- Have students make a written list of what they know: "List the types of foods that make up the food pyramid."

♦ Ask students to generate questions that they want answered before they begin to work on the task.

♦ Conduct an oral quiz, calling on students with a range of ability.

ACCESS

Now you must help students gain access to new knowledge. As explained in Chapter 6, acquiring new knowledge is a key part of solving problems and completing open-ended tasks. The benchmarks and the unit plan help you identify such knowledge. After identifying the knowledge, decide on the means of access: How will the students acquire the new knowledge? If you have the requisite materials and the preparation time, it is wise to provide alternative means for students who do not have strong verbal skills. Such students can learn from videos, computer software, audiotapes, and peer tutoring.

FACILITATE TASK PERFORMANCE

Having acquired the knowledge, students should be ready to perform the task. Initially, you would guide them through the process, gradually turning over control to the students. To guard against the use of activity for activity's sake, ask yourself this question: "Are they learning what they need to learn in order to accomplish the task?" From time to time, remind students of the performance task, to ensure that they understand the linkages between the activity and the task.

If you have planned a unit, as suggested in Chapter 6, then you should find it relatively simple to teach to the task. If you did not, then you should do a knowledge/skills analysis of the performance task.

Consider this example. Here is a fourth-grade U.S. history benchmark (as identified by Kendall & Marzano, 1997, p. 125): "understands how regional folk heroes and other popular figures have contributed to the cultural history of the U.S."

Here is the performance task one group of fourth-grade teachers devised.

Each group will look up and present to the class the important information about one of our heroes from the past. Be sure it is accurate information. One person in the group will tell the class the main facts of that hero's life. The others in the group will put on a short play. The play should illustrate one important incident in the hero's life. One person in each group will explain to the class why we remember that hero. Each member of the class will make a chart showing how all the heroes presented were similar to and different from each other.

To prepare students to accomplish this task successfully, you would make a *skills/knowledge analysis*. You would ask yourself this question: "What skills and knowledge will the students need to accomplish this task?" Then, once you have identified that comprehensive analysis, you would ask yourself, "Which of these skills and knowledge do all the students already have, and which will I have to teach to the class?" You would also note those skills and knowledge not mastered by some of the students, who will need some individual help.

Figure 8.1 shows how the fourth-grade team completed these analyses. They used the results to determine what they had to teach, what the students could learn from each other, and what skills needed only to be reinforced.

FIGURE 8.1. SKILLS/KNOWLEDGE ANALYSIS

Skill/Knowledge	Know	Learn
1. Locate sources.	X	
2. Take notes from sources.	X	
3. Narrate facts.	X	
4. Write, present short play.		X
5. Make comparison/contrast chart.		X
6. Know important facts about hero's life.		X
7. Analyze contributions of hero.		X

CONDUCT PERFORMANCE ASSESSMENT

As explained more fully in the next chapter, the unit would close with you making a summative assessment of how well the students completed the performance task.

USE CONTINUING PROCESSES TO ASSIST STUDENTS

Throughout the sequence of steps explained above, use the following processes as they seem necessary.

REPRESENT

This step is a reminder to ask students from time to time to *represent* their knowledge. Representing knowledge is a process of taking knowledge that has been formulated in a verbal form and translating it into an alternative form—usually a visual one. Such transformations are sometimes called *visual tools* or *graphic organizers*. Here are some of the alternative forms that can be used: flow chart; matrix; set of boxes with arrows showing relationships; web diagram; concept map; tree diagram. As both an example of representations and as an aid to your own comprehension, Figure 8.2 (p. 112) is offered as a visual representation of how to use ADI in the classroom. In the left-hand column, the figure shows the processes that go on throughout the act of learning; in the right-hand column are the steps that the teacher would undertake, in sequence.

Three commonly used representations are shown in Figures 8.3 (p. 113), 8.4 (p. 114), and 8.5 (p. 115). A tree map is used to show a clearly ordered hierarchical relationship. A web diagram is used to show multiple interactive forces. A Venn diagram visually represents the relationship of two concepts.

If you do not wish to teach students to use a particular type of representation, you can achieve almost the same effect in a simpler fashion. Just ask students to draw a picture of their knowledge, as in this example:

> Draw a picture of the plot of *Julius Caesar*. Visualize it any way you wish, only be accurate. [After students have drawn their pictures:] Now let's share with each other how we visualized the plot.

(Text continues on page 115.)

FIGURE 8.2 ASSESSMENT-DRIVEN INSTRUCTION:
A CONCEPTUAL FRAMEWORK

Continuing Processes   *Steps in Sequence*

                                          Organize Class

Help Students Represent   Engage Students
Knowledge
Provide Scaffolding

                                          Activate Prior Knowledge

                                          Facilitate Access to New
                                          Knowledge

Provide Formative   Facilitate Task Performance
Feedback
Facilitate Metacognition

                                          Conduct Performance
                                          Assessment

FIGURE 8.3 TREE MAP: FEDERAL GOVERNMENT

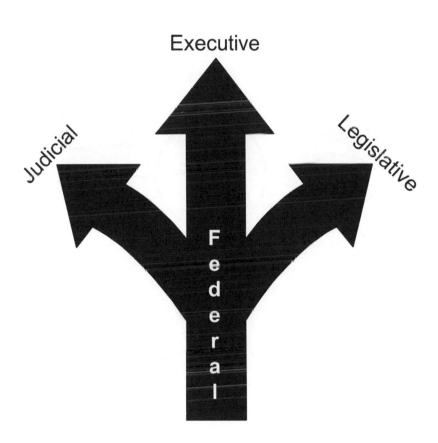

FIGURE 8.4 WEB DIAGRAM: PERSONAL INFLUENCES

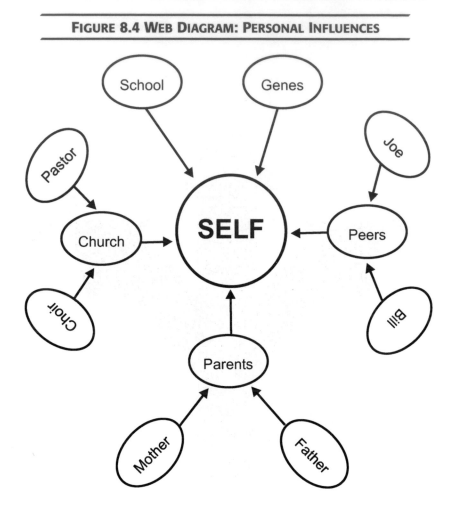

FIGURE 8.5 VENN DIAGRAM

Relationship: All husbands are male.

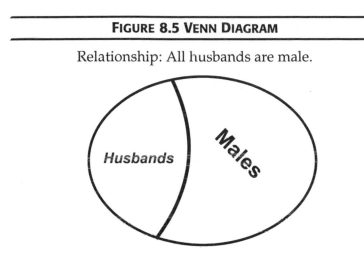

Several studies have found that the use of such representations improves reading comprehension. (See Pearson & Fielding, 1991.) These visual tools are also useful in problem solving, in organizing information, and in communicating with audiences. (For detailed information about the types and uses of such tools, see Hyerle, 1996.)

SCAFFOLD

As the students acquire knowledge and apply it to the performance task, keep in mind the importance of scaffolding. As explained previously, scaffolding can be generally understood as providing appropriate support and direction as the student works through the performance task. Scaffolding is a temporary bridge, as Figure 8.6 suggests, between you explaining everything and the students discovering everything on their own.

The literature reports several types of scaffolding as effective in helping students acquire complex mental operations (see Rosenshine & Meister, 1992):

♦ Half completed problems

The teacher would do the first step or two; the students would do the rest.

FIGURE 8.6. SCAFFOLDING STAGES

1. Teacher Dominates

    The teacher does all the work—explaining, telling, and modeling.

2. Teacher Scaffolds

    The teacher provides scaffolding as needed, decreasing it as students become more independent.

3. Students Scaffold

    Students use scaffolding strategies to help each other.

4. Students Operate Independently

    Students do all the work independently, with self-evaluation and peer and teacher feedback.

♦ Structured prompts

The teacher prepares and distributes a summary of the main steps in executing a process. Figure 8.7 is an example for writing a narrative.

♦ Teacher modeling and thinking aloud

The teacher models the step, thinking aloud as an example for the student.

♦ Cue cards

The teacher prepares and distributes small cards containing cues, hints, or suggestions.

♦ Self-checking procedures

The teacher helps the students perform self-evaluations, using the rubrics previously prepared.

As you use scaffolding, keep in mind the ultimate goal of enabling students to become self-directed learners.

FIGURE 8.7. STRUCTURED PROMPT:
WRITING THE NARRATIVE

In writing the personal narrative, keep these suggestions in mind:

- Describe the setting and show how it impacts upon you as the central character.
- Focus on the major conflict, portraying it in great detail.
- Use dialog to increase interest.
- Describe main characters in depth, using vivid images and descriptive language.
- Reflect about what you learned from the experience.

PROVIDE FORMATIVE FEEDBACK

As the students perform the task, monitor their work and give them constructive feedback as needed. Here are some questions to ask as you monitor students accessing knowledge and carrying out the task:

- Is their acquired knowledge accurate and current?
- Are all students sharing equally in their responsibilities?
- Are all students on task?
- Are they accomplishing the task at an appropriate pace?
- Are they demonstrating high quality performance?
- Do they need additional scaffolding?

MONITOR COGNITION

At appropriate times during the unit, you should help students monitor and reflect about their own thought processes and problem-solving strategies. Doing so is usually termed *metacognitive monitoring*, or, to put it simply, *thinking about thinking*. You can do this by asking students questions such as:

♦ How did you decide on the event you would dramatize?

♦ What other choices did you consider?

♦ What were you thinking at the time?

♦ How did you feel when you had finished?

Such metacognitive monitoring helps students understand their own and others' thinking processes and identify areas of strength and need.

A CONCLUDING NOTE

While the steps suggested above should be useful in most classes, you should modify the steps to suit your teaching style, your subject, and your students.

REFERENCES

Cotton, K. (1995). *Effective schooling practices: A research synthesis*, (1995 update). Portland, OR: Northwest Regional Educational Laboratory.

Gooding, K. (1994, April). *Teaching to the test: The influence of alternative modes of assessment on teachers' instructional strategies*. Paper presented at the annual meeting of the American Educational Research Association, New Orleans, LA.

Herman, J., & Golan, S. (1991). *Effects of standardized tests on teaching and learning* (CSE Technical Report #334). Los Angeles: National Center for Research on Evaluation, Standards, and Student Testing.

Hyerle, D. (1996). *Visual tools for constructing knowledge*. Alexandria, VA: Association for Supervision and Curriculum Development.

Kattri, N., Kane, M. B., & Reeve, A. L. (1995). How performance assessments affect teaching and learning. *Educational Leadership, 53* (3), 80–83.

9

CONDUCTING PERFORMANCE ASSESSMENTS

You should be ready now to conduct the performance assessment, a critical step in the entire process. As the term implies, a *performance assessment* is an evaluation of the students' performance in completing the performance task. This chapter suggests a process to use in making valid assessments.

DETERMINE THE PURPOSE OF THE PERFORMANCE ASSESSMENT

The first step is to determine the purposes for making such assessments. Here are several to consider (McTighe & Ferrara, 1997):

- ◆ Diagnose student strengths and problems. The assessment can give you some useful data about strengths you can build on and weaknesses you can remedy.
- ◆ Give feedback to students. The assessment can provide you with an opportunity to give students specific feedback that will help them improve subsequent performance.
- ◆ Modify your teaching. The assessment will also give you some feedback about your own teaching, suggesting how you might modify your instructional practices.
- ◆ Motivate student learning. A well-designed performance assessment can increase student motivation to learn, because many of the assessments will give students an opportunity to demonstrate to their peers what they have learned.

♦ Assign a grade. Although many teachers see the grading process as the main reason for making an assessment, keep in mind that a good assessment can serve many other purposes.

♦ Evaluate the curriculum. A valid assessment can also provide useful information to you and to administrators about the quality of the curriculum. If most students perform poorly on the assessment, the curriculum might be the problem.

The best assessments serve several purposes. Remember to give top priority to the learning-centered purposes.

IDENTIFY THE ASSESSORS

As the teacher, you play a key role in the assessment process. However, you should consider using others to complement your assessment. First, you should give special attention to student self-assessment. Student self-assessments can provide useful data if two conditions prevail. First, the students should be informed that the self-assessments will count as only one component of the assessment process. Second, students should be given appropriate training and feedback regarding how to assess their own performance. The best way to accomplish this is to take time to critically analyze their self-assessments, pointing out where and why your evaluations differ from theirs.

In addition to self-assessments, you should make appropriate use of peer assessments. Typically, peers will render assessments that are too generous, because they are reluctant to criticize other students. You can reduce such *assessment inflation* if you emphasize the need for constructive feedback in the learning process. You also should help students understand the characteristics of constructive feedback, as explained below. Finally, you should train the students in how to use the criteria and the rubrics as a way of making constructive assessments.

From time to time, you may also use other educators as assessors: other teachers in the school; teachers in other schools (including those at a distance, who communicate by e-mail); district and school administrators; and support staff, such as counselors and nurses.

Finally, it is appropriate to use parents and other citizens from the community to assess student performance. Obviously, parents should not evaluate the performance of their own children, but they can be trained to evaluate other students. Other citizens from the community, who have expertise in the area addressed by the assessment, can be a valuable resource. For example, if students were asked to write a letter to a town official, then the most realistic assessor is a town official.

DETERMINE THE FORM OF THE PERFORMANCE ASSESSMENT

If you have not already done so, you should determine the form of the assessment—what students will do to demonstrate that they have successfully completed the performance task and have acquired the associated learning. Here you have several options; the major types are explained briefly, as follows. (The typology is one suggested by McTighe & Ferrara, 1997.)

CONSTRUCTED RESPONSES

Although some experts frown on any brief response, having students construct a brief answer may be a useful means of checking student knowledge of terms and concepts. Constructing a response, such as writing a definition or drawing a conceptual map, is more valid than selecting the right answer from among four choices or matching a term with its definition. The chief drawback to short answers is that they do not provide an opportunity for in-depth analysis.

PRODUCTS

Several types of student products can play a useful part in the assessment process:

   ♦ Essay answer

   An essay answer can provide the student with an opportunity to explain an issue in depth or argue a point of view. The major limitation is that the essay has a note of unreality about it.

♦ Library paper, research report, or laboratory report

Although these terms are often used interchangeably, consider teaching students these distinctions: A *library paper* is a synthesis of knowledge that has been retrieved from available sources. Although library papers can teach students some useful information-processing skills, they do not provide an opportunity for student originality or creativity, too often leading to plagiarism. A *research report* is a report of the student's own investigations, building upon an existing knowledge base. If a student synthesizes the available information about cloning, that would be a library paper. If a student surveys and reports on student attitudes about cloning, the results would be presented in a research report. A *laboratory report* is a special type of research report, reporting on a scientific experiment that has been done to discover or confirm a scientific principle. You should minimize the use of library papers, emphasizing research reports instead.

♦ Log or journal

Having students keep a learning log or learning journal can be a useful way to assess student thought processes and problem-solving strategies. The log or journal can be especially useful as a means for establishing individual accountability. You need to monitor the log or journal in process, because many students seem to be reluctant journal-keepers.

♦ Portfolio or exhibit

The portfolio is one of the best ways for the student to show work in progress. The portfolio has been used successfully in assessing performance in both writing and mathematics, even though the assessors did not always agree with each other about ratings (Mills, 1996). The chief limitation of many portfolios is that they include only a self-selected sample, slanted, of course, to make the best impression. The art or science exhibit is a type of visual portfolio and serves the same purpose.

♦ Creative work

Having students write a story, play, or poem is a good way to stimulate creativity. Such creative work should be presented in a class publication or performance. Keep two cautions in mind: First, ensure that the creative product has a sound knowledge base and is not simply an "off-the-wall" response, and second, edit the publication or preview the dramatization to ensure that it does not violate school policies or community norms.

♦ Audio- or videotape

The effective production of an audio- or a videotape requires the mastery and application of several skills; however, making these records can be a very time-consuming process.

PERFORMANCES AND DEMONSTRATIONS

Several types of public performances and demonstrations can be useful measures of student achievement. A group oral report can both assess learning and inform other students. A science demonstration can accomplish the same purpose. A dramatic reading or enactment can increase the interest of both performers and audience. Debates can stimulate student interest, but they tend to polarize attitudes around complex issues that go beyond a simple pro or con stance.

PROCESSES

A process assessment attempts to help the student reflect about and report on processes used in completing the performance task or solving the problem. Process assessment can include these specific types:

♦ Observing students at work.

♦ Interviewing students during and after task completion.

- Asking students to keep a running record of their thought processes as they solve the problem or complete the task.
- Asking students to describe their processes in a brief report.

CHOOSING THE ASSESSMENT TYPE

Three criteria are important in selecting one or more of these types: validity, reliability, and feasibility. The criterion of *validity* asks, "Does it really measure the student's achievement with the performance task?" The criterion of *reliability* asks, "Will the evaluation produce consistent results?" The criterion of *feasibility* asks, "Can it be effectively executed in the classroom, in the time available?"

REVIEW AND EXPLAIN THE RUBRICS

Each assessor should receive a copy of the rubrics, along with a clear explanation of how to use them in making the assessment. It is hoped that the students themselves have received the rubrics at the outset, when they were embarking upon the performance task.

MAKE FORMATIVE ASSESSMENTS BY MONITORING STUDENT PROGRESS

As the students work on the performance task, monitor their progress and give them formative feedback as needed. Be alert to these developing problems and take the corrective actions needed:

- Students seem confused about the performance task.
- Individual members of the group are not contributing to group progress.
- Group is having problems getting organized for action.
- Students have not developed the knowledge base sufficiently.

♦ Students have not mastered a required strategy.

♦ Student progress is hampered by absences and interruptions.

MAKE THE SUMMATIVE
PERFORMANCE ASSESSMENT

With these steps completed, you should be ready to make the final performance assessment, using the rubrics already developed. The following guidelines should be useful:

♦ In general, make a holistic assessment and then analyze the individual components with the rubrics in mind. A *holistic assessment* is an overall judgment of the quality of the performance. An *analytic rating* examines the quality of the individual parts. After making the analytic judgment, you may see the need to modify your overall evaluation.

♦ Assess in terms of the standards you expect, not on the basis of how one student compares with another. "Grading on the curve" decreases student motivation and results in invalid assessments.

♦ Don't change the rules in the middle of the game. If you have developed rubrics, have informed students about them, and have taught with them in mind, then you should not change or add to them during the assessment process, even if you realize that they could be improved.

♦ Give students constructive feedback. *Constructive feedback* does not attack the person; it is timely; it is data-based and specific; it suggests how work can be improved. Contrast these two examples:

  • *Destructive Feedback:* "Bill, you messed up on that assignment. Your letter is boring; it says the same old things. Why don't you rewrite it?"

  • *Constructive Feedback.* "Bill, I did not feel personally connected with your letter. I always begin to read a letter wondering why I should give it my attention. How do you think you might write the letter so that it makes contact with the reader?"

SOLICIT STUDENT FEEDBACK

After you have completed the performance assessment, you should solicit and use student feedback, to improve future assessments. Here are some questions you can ask students in a survey or class discussion:

- Did the assessment help you learn?
- Did the assessment provide you with constructive suggestions for improvement?
- Was the assessment valid? Did it really measure your learning?
- Was the assessment interesting? Did you find personal value in it?

A CONCLUDING NOTE

Assessment is not an optional extra for good teachers. It is, instead, an integral part of the entire learning process.

REFERENCES

McTighe, J., & Ferrara, S. (1997). *Assessing learning in the classroom.* Washington, DC: National Education Association.

Mills, R. P. (1996). Statewide portfolio assessment: The Vermont experience. In J. B. Baron & D. P. Wolf (Eds.), *Performance-based student assessment: Challenges and possibilities* (pp. 192–215). Chicago: University of Chicago Press.

10

REMEDIATING LEARNING

Despite your best efforts in designing and assessing performance tasks, there are always some students who do not
achieve at the level that they should. Those students need both
on-the-spot and postassessment remediation. After explaining
the kind of classroom environment needed, the chapter examines both of these approaches.

ESTABLISHING A LEARNING-CENTERED ENVIRONMENT

Any type of remediation is more effective if it is implemented in a learning-centered environment—a classroom
where all students are expected to learn and are given the help
they need to achieve. Such a climate is established when both
you and the students hold and act upon these beliefs:

- All students can achieve mastery.

   This, of course, is the basic belief—that all students
   can achieve at the expected level. Some will need
   more time or additional help—but all can achieve.

- All learning involves mistakes and errors.

   Error-free learning is rare. The goal for both the
   teacher and the students is to learn from error, correct the mistakes, and move on to new learning.

- Learning is a shared responsibility.

   Students, their parents, and the teacher are all partners in the learning enterprise. If students are not
   achieving at the expected level, the three partners
   should collaborate in diagnosing the problem and
   finding a remedy.

- At some time, in some area, everyone needs help.

  Each of us has some talent strengths and some talent weaknesses. We all learn by helping each other.

- We learn by asking questions.

  The only foolish questions are those that are not asked.

- Success comes from a combination of ability plus effort.

  Neither alone is sufficient; students who do not succeed should analyze both the ability they brought to the task and the effort they expended.

You can establish this climate by modeling the behaviors implied, by affirming them as you teach, and by rewarding students who model those values.

PROVIDING ON-THE-SPOT REMEDIATION

On-the-spot remediation is the response you make in every lesson as students indicate both verbally and nonverbally that they are having difficulty understanding. This kind of remediation requires ongoing monitoring of learning and adjustment of instruction.

MONITORING STUDENT LEARNING WHEN WORKING IN GROUPS ON A PERFORMANCE TASK

Monitoring a group at work on a performance task is especially helpful. Here are some techniques that will give you useful information:

- Observe to analyze the group interactions.

  Watch especially for the following problems: one student is dominating the work; one or more students seem to be passive; the group seems off task; two or more members seem to be in conflict; the group do not seem to be taking the task seriously.

♦ Observe to assess their understanding and use of the knowledge base.

Watch students as they retrieve information–are they locating the best resources? Observe for signs of reading problems, such as a slow pace of reading or lip movement.

♦ Observe students as they make decisions about the task.

Note whether students are making unwise decisions as they work at the task. Check the progress they are making towards task completion.

♦ At the end of the class session, ask students to report briefly on what they accomplished and what difficulties they encountered.

♦ Evaluate student products.

As students produce pieces of the solution or drafts of written assignments, provide constructive feedback—either from you or from peer tutors. The rubrics are helpful here.

MONITORING STUDENT LEARNING IN WHOLE-CLASS INSTRUCTION

When providing whole-class instruction, you need to monitor learning closely. Here are some strategies to keep in mind:

♦ Ask questions to check on learning.

Expert teachers use two strategies in asking questions—group alerting and targeted solicitation. *Group alerting* is asking a question and then calling on someone. Here are examples to show the difference.

- *Group Alerting:* "Why do you think we became deeply involved in Vietnam? Bill, what do you think?"

- *Individual Alerting:* "Bill, why do you think we became involved in Vietnam?"

The problem with individual alerting is that all the rest of the class relax, knowing that Bill has been called on. When the teacher uses group alerting, almost everyone begins to think about the question.

When teachers use *targeted solicitation*, they call on specific students whom they wish to engage, rather than relying upon volunteers. Relying on volunteers often yields misleading information, since you are not getting a representative sample.

♦ Encourage student questions.

In the typical classroom, the teacher asks almost all the questions—and student questions, when they are asked, are gamelike, designed to distract the teacher from the planned lesson. In a learning-centered classroom, the students frequently ask real questions to clear up their confusion or extend their knowledge.

♦ Probe incorrect answers—the probing gives you some clues about the nature and cause of the error.

If a student gives an incorrect answer, it is sometimes helpful to probe for the reasons, rather than calling on someone else or simply indicating that the answer is wrong. The student may have misunderstood the question, used the wrong information, or operated on the material in an illogical manner.

Here is an example of a student error.

$$437 - 269 = 232$$

The student probably is using an incorrect algorithm—"always subtract the smaller number from the larger one."

♦ Use writing to assess and facilitate learning.

You can give a brief written quiz. You can also ask students to write their answers before discussing them. The writing process enables them to reflect about their knowledge and prepare their responses.

RESPONDING TO STUDENTS' ERRORS

First, consider how you might differentiate your response based on the number of students making the mistake. If one or two students seem to be confused, respond to them individually while the rest of the class is engaged in some other learning activity. If a group of students seems to be in error, work with them as a group during whatever time is available. If most of the class seems confused, take the time to provide a special remedial session.

You should also use the monitoring data to adjust your instruction. Remedial adjustments can take several forms:

- Use a simpler vocabulary; abstract technical terms often give students trouble.

- Give more examples of concepts.

   The examples will often clarify confusion about the concept. Younger students will also need hands-on experiences to understand concepts.

- Use visual aids to represent complex concepts and processes—pictures, diagrams, and sketches.

- Slow the pace of learning.

   Because time allocated and learning accomplished are closely related, slowing the pace and providing additional time often helps.

- Use more able students as tutors—but do not exploit the gifted by using them too often as tutors.

- Provide additional scaffolding.

   Often students are not learning because the teacher has not provided sufficient structure and assistance. Additional scaffolding includes such strategies as modeling, demonstrating, providing incomplete problems, and giving students cue cards.

PROVIDING POSTASSESSMENT REMEDIATION

Postassessment remediation occurs after a performance assessment has been made. You have made an assessment of student performance and find that some students did not achieve at the expected level. In response, you diagnose the problem and provide postassessment remediation.

DIAGNOSING THE PROBLEM

Begin diagnosing the problem by reviewing the results of the performance assessment. Also reflect about the on-the-spot remediation you provided, because many problems are of a cumulative nature. It is also helpful to interview students who have not performed well, to elicit their perceptions about their problems. In making these analyses, Figure 10.1 is useful. It lists the likely causes of poor performance. The list is intended to remind you of the several explanations for poor performance. Some teachers are inclined to blame the students; many students blame the teacher. An objective diagnosis is needed, not blaming and making excuses.

PROVIDING REMEDIATION

Obviously the diagnosis will suggest the focus of your remediation efforts. If insufficient scaffolding seems to have been the problem, then provide students with the additional structure they need as they work their way through the task again. Here is a general remediation strategy that seems to work.

First, group the students who did not perform well, unless most of the class experienced major difficulties. Arrange for them to have additional time—before school, after school, or during the regular period while the rest of the class are working on an enrichment unit. (See the next chapter for suggestions about enrichment.) Then, reteach as necessary, using student tutors who have been trained to provide the remediation needed. If you do the reteaching, provide alternative methods of learning. If students had to read to acquire the knowledge base in the initial attempt, provide visual sources in the reteaching.

If the original learning process used a discovery approach in which students had to generate knowledge, consider using a direct-instruction model for the remediation. In the direct-instruction model, the teacher explains, checks on understanding, and provides guided and independent practice. A significant body of research attests to the effectiveness of direct instruction when it is correctly implemented (Adams & Engelmann, 1996).

FIGURE 10.1. LIKELY CAUSES OF POOR PERFORMANCE

Home Environment

- Student had a home environment that was not conducive to learning.

Classroom Climate

- Students were frequently off-task.
- Several students were disruptive.
- Students exerted pressure on each other not to achieve.

Curriculum

- Curriculum was developmentally inappropriate.
- Curriculum did not seem to connect with students.

Performance Task, Rubrics, and Performance Assessment

- Performance task was unclear.
- Performance task was too difficult.
- Rubrics were inappropriate.
- Performance assessment was not carried out appropriately.

Group Interactions

- Group experienced conflict.
- Group lacked effective leadership.
- Group norms did not support academic achievement.

Students

- Students did not devote sufficient time because they were absent or excused.
- Students seemed to lack motivation and did not believe they could succeed.
- Students had learning disabilities.
- Students were deficient in the key skills required.

♦ Students used ineffective strategies in taking tests and attacking problems.

Access to Knowledge Base

♦ Means of access was not appropriate for students; for example, too much reading was required for students with poor reading ability.

♦ Materials were deficient—inaccurate, dated, superficial, or too difficult

Instruction

♦ Pace of instruction was too fast.

♦ Insufficient scaffolding was provided.

♦ Instruction was not focused on the performance task.

♦ Required learning strategies were not taught.

For students who fail persistently, you may need to implement a more comprehensive approach. Researchers in the field identify such students as suffering from a *failure syndrome*, an attitude of expecting and being accustomed to failure, thus setting low goals for themselves and blaming their lack of ability for poor performance. (The term *failure syndrome* and the following discussion are derived from Good & Brophy, 1997.) In working with such students, experts recommend an intensive approach that embodies these strategies:

♦ Provide support and encouragement throughout the learning process, ensuring such students that they can succeed and that you will help them succeed.

♦ Teach them how to cope with learning difficulties: concentrate on the task, rather than worrying about failure; when encountering problems with learning, retrace the steps to find the mistake, or to take a different approach.

♦ When they experience failure, help them analyze the problem; looking for such causes as inadequate effort, lack of information, or use of ineffective strategies, rather than lack of ability.

♦ Use their mistakes to teach them how to remedy their own learning, identifying points of difficulty and analyzing where they went astray.

♦ Help them set reasonably high expectations for themselves; do not accept shoddy work that suggests they did not make the necessary effort.

♦ Provide counseling where needed, to ensure that students understand the connection with present academic success and future career success. In doing so, enlist the support of parents.

To understand the importance of remediation, consider this instructional problem. You developed a performance task that required students to understand the importance of regional folk heroes. (See Figure 8.1, page 110, for the skill/knowledge analysis for this task.) In your assessment of their performance on the task, you determine that about half the class has not developed a clear and accurate comparison/contrast chart. You decide to provide remediation for those not performing satisfactorily, while the rest of the class complete a self-directed enrichment unit on folk heroes of today. You begin the remediation by reviewing their work and asking them questions to determine the reason for their unsatisfactory performance. Your analysis indicates that they had problems in identifying the elements to be used in the comparison/contrast chart. You remember that you treated this topic only briefly. You decide to reteach, by using examples of concepts they know well, such as elementary school and middle school. You prepare a cue card to remind them of the mental steps to take in identifying the elements to be compared. You make a final assessment of the effectiveness of the review work.

Pitfalls in Providing Remediation

In providing remediation, remember to avoid these pitfalls:

- Do not label or stigmatize those needing help. Emphasize that all learners need help at some time, in some areas.
- Do not blame the students, the parents, or yourself. Adopt a problem-solving approach instead.
- Do not simply provide more of the same. If a given method did not work initially with some of the students, try a different approach.
- Do not decrease the amount of time they spend on regular instruction; "pull-out" programs are ineffective (Jakubowski & Ogletree, 1993).
- Do not give up on students. Believe in your own power to ultimately reach all.

References

Adams, G. L., & Engelmann, S. (1996). *Research on direct instruction: 25 years beyond DISTAR.* Seattle, WA: Educational Achievement Systems.

Good, T. L., & Brophy, J. E. (1997). *Looking in classrooms* (7th ed.). New York: Longman.

Jakubowski, D., & Ogletree, E. J. (1993). *The effectiveness of Chapter 1 pull-out programs on math achievement.* Education Document Reproduction Service No. ED 367 734.

11

PROVIDING ENRICHMENT

This work has assumed that standards-based curricula and their related tasks and assessments will occupy no more than 80 percent of the classroom time available. This recommendation is an attempt to give you some "wiggle room" and to enable you to have sufficient time for remediation and enrichment. The previous chapter explained how you can provide remediation; this chapter examines the enrichment curriculum.

UNDERSTANDING THE ENRICHMENT CURRICULUM

Enrichment is used here to mean units of study that go beyond the required written curriculum. They provide greater depth to the required curriculum by more deeply exploring topics that are covered only superficially in the required curriculum. Suppose, for example, that the required curriculum emphasized the study of Shakespearean tragedy; an enrichment unit might include an analysis of the nature of tragedy and the differences between Greek and Elizabethan tragedy. Enrichment units provide greater breadth to the required curriculum, by examining topics related to those in the required curriculum. For example, teachers might develop a unit on the way theatrical stages affected the development of drama, as a means of broadening the unit on Shakespearean tragedy. Or an enrichment unit might introduce students to a topic not even referred to in the required curriculum, such as the history of the local town and its environs. In each case, the enrichment curriculum is teacher-developed and teacher-evaluated—with student input.

UNDERSTANDING THE DEBATE
OVER THE ENRICHED CURRICULUM

Some critics question the value of the enrichment curriculum. Most critics point out that it takes time away from the study of the required curriculum. Some question the ability of teachers to develop curricula. They fear that enrichment units will only be collections of entertaining activities. Others take an elitist position, arguing that enrichment units should be provided solely to the academically gifted.

While acknowledging that such concerns have some legitimacy, the position taken here is that well-designed enrichment units have value from both the teacher's and the students' perspectives. They restore some curricular control to the teacher, who otherwise might feel that he or she is a slave to the required curriculum—or a mere mechanic delivering what someone else has produced. Because enrichment units are not part of state or district accountability programs, they allow the teacher greater creativity and freedom. Thus, they provide an ideal mechanism for teachers who wish to experiment with new ways of learning or new types of units. They enable the teacher to bring to the classroom the teacher's own special knowledge, talents, and enthusiasms; such personalized connections to the curriculum usually result in better teaching. Finally, they enable the teacher to localize the curriculum—to use local resources and to respond to the special needs of the students in that classroom.

RELATING ENRICHMENT UNITS TO PERFORMANCE
TASKS AND ASSESSMENTS

While the use of enrichment units is intended to give you greater freedom in the planning and teaching of these units, serious consideration should be given to making them performance task-focused, especially when you are beginning to experiment with performance assessment. One complex performance task, with its associated performance assessment, can well constitute the essence of an enrichment unit. Suppose, for example, that you and your colleagues wanted to teach an enrichment unit for high school juniors on college selection. You might construct a performance task of this sort:

> Your goal is to identify five colleges that represent your best choices to explore before making a final decision. In your college selection portfolio, include these elements:
>
> - An explanation of the process you used in narrowing your selections, including the use of computerized data bases.
> - A profile of the five colleges you have tentatively selected, including the features that especially attracted you.
> - A letter requesting a summer tour of the campus and an interview.
> - The questions you would like to have answered in the campus visit.

That performance task would then be used to structure the enrichment course.

Here is another example. This one is based on the following fourth-grade arts benchmark: "Identifies people, events, time, and place in classroom dramatizations."

> You are to write and produce a classroom play. The play should center around a conflict involving 3 people or characters: one boy, age 10; his sister, age 12; and their mother or father. The setting of the play should be the family home, in the morning before going to school. You should write the script, telling the characters what to say. You should also present or produce the play. It should last no more than 15 minutes.

Using performance tasks as the basis of enrichment units has several advantages. From your perspective, it gives additional opportunities to experiment with task-based instruction in a less-pressure context. It enables you to contribute to the curriculum in a very significant way. It becomes a key part of your own professional development. From the students' perspective, it gives them additional practice and instruction in using knowledge to solve problems. It extends their experience in making knowledge generative by actively using it. And it reminds them that task-focused learning can be exciting and enriching.

DEVELOPING A PLAN FOR ENRICHMENT UNITS

In planning enrichment units, it is essential that you work with colleagues teaching the same subject at different levels, to ensure that there is no repetition in the subject matter of enrichment units, thereby avoiding the student complaint: "We did dinosaurs last year." Team planning is also more likely to lead to a higher standard of quality.

A four-phase planning process is recommended. The first phase is the organizational meeting with colleagues that should address basic structural issues. First, consider the delivery mechanism or structure for enrichment. One option is for each teacher to teach his or her own enrichment units, any time that he or she wishes. The enrichment thus becomes an extension of the regular class. The other option is to structure the enrichment units as minicourses that meet for a few weeks. In this option, students are given a list of courses and teachers and make their choices in consultation with their parents. These elective minicourses seem especially popular in middle schools, where there seem to be fewer pressures to adhere closely to the required curriculum.

Also at this first meeting, deal with the issue of time. How much time should be allocated to these units? What time frame will be used—before school, after school, during a special class period, or in special *enrichment weeks* carved out of the regular school calendar? Finally, you should decide on the issue of staffing enrichment courses. Some schools report success in using experts from the community, parents, central office supervisors, school administrators, older students, university faculty, and teacher aides. Others limit the instructional staff to certified teachers.

In the second phase, each teacher develops a tentative list of unit titles. The unit titles should reflect the content of the unit and can be drawn from several sources:

- Learning materials.

  If you have access to an excellent video series, such as the Ken Burns documentary on the Civil War, you could build a unit around it.

- Local resources.

  Local museums, libraries, laboratories, and cultural centers might suggest interesting topics for a unit. Studying local history, regional dialects, and local place names is also a good way to capitalize upon community resources.

- Special student interests.

  Students' special interests in such areas as photography, aeronautics, trains, contemporary music, football, and food can be a useful source of enrichment.

- Teachers' special interests.

  Your own hobbies can provide a sound basis for enrichment units.

- New developments in the disciplines.

  Science especially continues to develop new knowledge that is not yet incorporated into the required curriculum.

- Disciplines not included in the required program of studies.

  The social sciences are an especially fertile field, because disciplines such as sociology, anthropology, and psychology are usually not included in the required curriculum and offer excellent opportunities for enrichment.

- The required curriculum.

  Topics that extend or deepen the required curriculum should also be considered.

In considering possible topics, give special attention to the possibilities offered by curriculum integration. Many interesting topics will draw from two or more subjects, such as these:

The Changing Family; Solving Community Problems: Towards a Better Future; Making, Spending, and Saving Money.

This second phase of the planning process is also a good time to secure student input. Some teachers have found it useful to survey student interests or to take a class period to solicit their suggestions.

When this second phase is completed, you and your colleagues should confer and develop a final list of offerings by synthesizing each teacher's contributions. In developing such a list, your group should apply these criteria:

Does the final set of offerings...

♦ Avoid repetition from grade to grade? (Note, however, that some units may provide for multigrade enrollment.)

♦ Reflect students' developmental needs and abilities?

♦ Avoid content that would create undue community controversy?

♦ Enrich and go beyond the required curriculum?

♦ Provide sufficiently for curriculum integration?

The final phase of planning involves the development of the unit plan or the course syllabus. Either working together or individually, the team develop plans for each enrichment unit or course. Because these enrichment units or courses are not included in the high-stakes testing program, you have greater latitude in the planning process. There are two practical options. For some units or courses, a list of topics should suffice. An example is provided in Figure 11.1. In other instances, you might find that a fully described performance task, the rubrics, and an explanation of the performance assessment would be more useful. An example is shown in Figure 11.2.

AVOIDING PITFALLS IN PROVIDING ENRICHMENT

Just because you are planning and teaching enrichment units is not a reason to sacrifice quality. Be aware of these cautions:

**FIGURE 11.1. EXAMPLE OF AN ENRICHMENT-
COURSE SYLLABUS**

Enrichment course title: Money—How to spend it and save it.
Number of class meetings: 6 periods
Topics:

1. Making a realistic budget.
2. Becoming a smart shopper.
3. What to do if you make a mistake in buying.
4. Saving for college.
5. Saving for long-term goals.
6. Establishing and maintaining good credit.

**FIGURE 11.2. PERFORMANCE TASK FOR
ENRICHMENT UNIT**

Enrichment course title: Money—How to spend it and save it.
Number of class meetings: 6 periods
Performance task:

Develop your Financial Portfolio. It must include the
following:

1. A budget for the next 6 months.
2. A brochure explaining to middle school students
    how they should shop for clothing.
3. An explanation of what you would do if you found
    that a product you had just bought was defective.
4. A plan you develop with your parent(s) showing
    how you will save for education beyond high
    school.
5. A long-term financial plan showing how you will
    save for the long term.
6. A letter to a credit bureau requesting a copy of your
    credit report.

- Do not turn enrichment into "fun and games." Enrichment units should be interesting, but they should also embody quality learning.

- Avoid activities just for the sake of activities. Be sure they are linked with enrichment outcomes.

- Continue to hold students accountable for completing tasks, doing assigned homework, and staying on task during classroom work. Enrichment should not mean relax and take it easy.

- Do not forget about the importance of evaluation. Give students ongoing feedback. Use the rubrics to evaluate their performance. And be sure to evaluate the enrichment units themselves.

12

PUTTING IT ALL TOGETHER

To help you see the big picture as all the pieces are put together, this chapter reviews the main steps in the assessment-driven instruction system and presents, for each component, an example to illustrate the process. Keep in mind that this book focuses on the teacher's role in each of these functions. (For a fuller description of the processes used at the district level, see the companion work by this author, Glatthorn, 1998.)

STATE AND DISTRICT-LEVEL FOUNDATIONS

The state department of education and the district curriculum committee establish a foundation for your work as a teacher. For most teachers, the process begins at the state level, when the state department of education identifies content standards for each subject for Grades K-12. Most states also specify school-level benchmarks, the more specific components of standards. Here is an example of a standard and one of its benchmarks (from Kendall & Marzano, 1997, p. 134):

- *Standard:* Understands cultural and ecological interactions among previously unconnected people resulting from early European exploration and colonization.
- *Benchmark:* Level II (Grades 5–6)

  Knows the features of the major European exploration and colonization.

The school district uses that information to develop its own curriculum guide, with teacher input. The district curriculum guide includes the standards and the related benchmarks, as well as other components that the district decides are useful (such as suggested teaching and learning activities). A district curriculum committee should review the standards promulgated by the several professional groups to determine whether the district guide should include any of those professional standards. The district also makes decisions as to the subject emphasis for each grade. For example, the district might decide that in social studies, U.S. history should be taught in Grade 5 and world history in Grade 6.

IDENTIFY BENCHMARKS FOR
A SPECIFIC GRADE LEVEL

Now you and your colleagues become active in the process. The discussion that follows assumes that you are working with an instructional team, organized by grade level or by subject. To provide more specific guidance to teachers, when benchmarks are identified for a group of grades, you decide which benchmarks should be emphasized at a specific grade level.

In making this decision, keep in mind several guidelines. First, the standards-based curriculum should not require more than 80 percent of the time available, so as to provide time for remediation and enrichment. This means that you will probably identify 8 to 12 standards for each subject. For each standard, identify three to four benchmarks for each grade. In making the decision about grade level benchmarks, consider the subject emphasis, the students' cognitive development, the state tests, and any state-adopted textbooks.

Considering all these factors, the English language arts/social studies team decided to allocate the benchmark noted above (about European explorations) to Grade 5.

DEVELOP UNIT TITLES

The next step is to develop a tentative list of unit titles. First, review all the standards and benchmarks that you are expected to teach.

In doing so, keep in mind the importance of depth. To provide depth of understanding, you may have to be selective about the standards you can address. Here is an example of the problem you face. As noted above, some experts recommend that you structure your planning so that you teach 8 to 12 standards each year, for each subject. Yet the Kendall and Marzano compilation identifies 31 standards for U.S. history!

In deciding on the unit titles, also consider these factors: students' developmental needs and interests; the organizing structure of the textbook; the availability of other materials; and the content of state tests. Also reflect on the kinds of units (standards-focused, unified, or integrated—or a combination of the three).

DEVELOP LONG-TERM PLANS FOR TEACHING

The next step is to use that list of unit titles to develop long-term plans for teaching. Depending on how the school organizes the school year, the plans will cover a quarter, a term, or a school year. There are several steps to developing the plan. First note the significant events taking place in the school and community, such as national holidays and parents' nights. Decide on the length of each unit, balancing the need for depth with the accommodation to students' attention span. Then decide on the sequence of the units and the organizational pattern you will use, such as chronological or thematic. Enter all this information into a special form, noting the standards and benchmarks that the unit addresses.

In the example used here, the fifth grade team decided to develop standards-focused units that emphasized social studies, while integrating relevant aspects of English language arts. The significant parts of their term calendar are shown in Figure 12.1.

DESIGN PERFORMANCE TASKS

Now you are ready to take on perhaps the most critical task—designing the performance tasks. There are many ways to proceed. The one presented in this book includes the following steps.

First, review the standards, the benchmarks, and the long-term plan in order to determine the general emphasis of the task. In the example used here, the fifth grade teachers decided to develop a performance task for the first unit, "The Great Explorers." The planning calendar indicated that 12 lessons were

FIGURE 12.1. TERM PLANNING CALENDAR

Weeks	Important Events	Unit Title	Standards
9/7–9/25	Labor Day Rosh Hashanah Parents Night	The Great Explorers	Social studies: Std 2 Language arts: Std 4
9/28–10/16	Yom Kippur Columbus Day	Revolution and the new nation	Social studies: Stds 3 Language arts: Stds. 3, 5
10/19–11/6	Halloween Election Day Report cards	Expansion and reform	Social studies: Std. 4 Language arts: 1, 4
11/9–11/27	Veterans Day Thanksgiving	Civil War and Reconstruc-tion	Social studies: Std. 5 Language arts: Std. 11
11/30–12/18	Hanukkah	The Great Depression	Social studies: Std. 8 Language arts: Std. 11
1/3–1/21		The recent past and the present	Social studies: Stds. 9, 10 Language arts: Stds. 1, 4

Notes:
1. Each unit takes approximately 12 class sessions of 90 minutes each.
2. Each unit is followed by a 3-day period for enrichment and remediation.

allocated, with 3 additional lessons earmarked for enrichment and remediation. The calendar also indicated that the unit would deal with these standards, with the benchmarks noted:

- ◆ Social Studies:
  - Standard: 1. Understands cultural and ecological interactions among previously unconnected people resulting from early European exploration and colonization.
  - Benchmark: Knows the features of the major European explorations that took place between the 15th and 17th centuries (routes, motives, goals, achievements, problems, fears and superstitions, expectations) by the Spanish, French, Dutch, and English explorers.
- ◆ Language Arts:
  - Standard:4. Effectively gathers and uses information for research purposes.
  - Benchmark: Uses multiple representations of information to find information.

At this stage you might also wish to derive the classroom learning objectives, the very specific outcomes used in making daily lesson plans. For example, here is one learning objective derived from the social studies benchmark noted above:

Identify the routes of the Spanish explorers.

With this information in mind, do some brainstorming to get some preliminary ideas for the performance task, reflecting on several factors: the time available; the resources at hand; the classroom learning objectives; how students would demonstrate their knowledge; and the purpose of the assessment.

The first draft of the performance task can be a bit sketchy, as in this example of one part of the explorer benchmark:

Pretend that you are an explorer from one of the nations studied. Write a journal entry about the problems encountered, your fears and superstitions, and your expectations.

With the performance task tentatively sketched in, you should be ready to express your ideas in a scenario, a mental image of how the unit might proceed. Here, for example, is one scenario that might be developed for the example used here:

> Divide the class into groups—one for each group of explorers. Each group gets a copy of the relevant chapter from the book, *The Explorers*. For the explorers assigned, each group draws a map showing the route, produces a journal entry for problems, fears and superstitions, and expectations—and then develops an information matrix for the rest of the items. Then the class puts all that information together.

At this point you should be ready to assemble a detailed version of the performance task. Here is an example of the final draft of the explorers task:

> You will be assigned to a group representing either the Spanish, French, Dutch, or English explorers. Your group has several tasks. Each group first will draw a map showing the route taken. Second, you will pretend that you are one of the crew. You will write a journal entry expressing the problems you faced, your fears and superstitions, and what the captain hoped would be achieved by the voyage. Then your group will develop a simple chart, which will show the motives for the trip, the goals, and the achievements. Your group will then present its information to the class.

> After all groups have reported, each member of the class will be required to perform these tasks: draw a composite map showing all the routes taken; write a summary of the crews' problems, fears and superstitions, and expectations; and draw a special chart, called a matrix, showing the motives, goals, and achievements of each of the explorer groups.

You then should evaluate the performance task, revising as appropriate.

DEVELOP CRITERIA AND RUBRICS

To guide the student work and the assessment process, you should next identify the criteria and the rubrics. The criteria are the general features you will use in making the assessment. The rubrics specify the criteria, the levels of performance, and the indicators for each level.

Here are the criteria that might be used in the explorer task:

+ *For the group performance:* Accuracy of map; accuracy and detail of journal entry; accuracy of chart; effectiveness of writing.

+ *For individual performance:* Accuracy of composite map; accuracy of summary; accuracy of matrix; effectiveness of writing.

For each criterion, develop the necessary rubrics. Figure 12.2 shows the rubrics that the fifth grade team might develop for one of the criteria.

FIGURE 12.2. RUBRICS FOR ONE CRITERION

Criteria/ Levels	Superior	Good	Satisfactory	Unsatisfactory
Journal accuracy and detail	Accurate in all respects; well detailed	One minor error in content, with sufficient detail	Two or three minor errors in content; important details noted	One or more major errors; one or more minor errors; important details lacking

DEVELOP UNITS BASED ON PERFORMANCE TASKS

At this stage, it is helpful to develop a unit based on the performance task, although some teachers prefer to move directly to using assessment-driven instruction. If you decide to develop a unit, first review all the steps you have taken thus far, noting especially the unit title and the number of lessons allocated. Next, determine the knowledge students will need and how they will gain access to it. In the example given here, each group will need to know the following for its group: route; problems; fears and superstitions; expectations. They can get that knowledge by reading the book provided. Identify the learning strategy that you will use in the unit. In the example, you will teach the strategy of using a matrix to organize information. Then do a task analysis of the performance task, identify the assessments you will make, and record all the decisions in a unit-planning chart.

USE ASSESSMENT-DRIVEN INSTRUCTION

You have specified the task and the rubrics—and perhaps have developed a unit. Now you are ready to use assessment-driven instruction. While there is no single correct way of using this approach, these guidelines are useful:

- Organize the class in accordance with the group structures you have decided to use—whole class, individualized, small group, or a combination. In the example being used here, the teacher would decide to use a combination of all three.

- Engage the students in the task by helping them make connections with the performance task. If you were teaching the explorers unit, begin by asking students about contemporary explorers.

- Activate the students' prior knowledge in order to determine what students already know and how they understand the topic. In the example used here, the teacher might ask students to write what they already know about the explorers and then call for a whole-class response to such questions as these:

  - How many can name one explorer?

- How many know the countries of origin of the explorers?

- Enable the students to gain access to the knowledge they will need. The knowledge base is important. While the teacher is usually a good source of knowledge, you should also make available to the students such varied sources as the Internet, library books, and videocassettes. For the explorer task, each group would receive a copy of *The Explorers*, a nonfiction work written for intermediate-grade students. The teacher would also secure a video cassette about the voyages of the explorers.

- Facilitate task performance. This is perhaps the key step in assessment-driven instruction. Your job here is to prepare the students to do well in performing the task. In a sense, you teach to the task. If you have already developed a unit based on the performance task, you may just wish to implement the unit, assuring that you have prepared the students fully. If you have not developed a task-focused unit, you may find it helpful at this stage to make a skills/ knowledge analysis, similar to Figure 12.3. To complete the analysis, review the performance task. Then identify all the skills and knowledge that the students will need to complete the task successfully. Then, by reflecting about what you learned in having them activate prior knowledge, and by drawing upon your own knowledge of the students, indicate for each of the skills or knowledge items whether the students already know it or whether they need to learn it.

CONDUCT THE PERFORMANCE ASSESSMENT

Next, conduct the performance assessment, to determine the extent to which the students have successfully carried out the performance task. Here you will find the rubrics essential. In assessing student performance on the task, make two assess-

FIGURE 12.3. SKILLS/KNOWLEDGE ANALYSIS

Skills/Knowledge	Know	Learn
1. Draw a map.	X	
2. Write a journal entry.	X	
3. Develop a chart.	X	
4. Know route of one group of explorers.		X
5. Know problems, fears and superstitions, expectations, motives, goals, achievements of group assigned.		X
6. Draw composite map.		X
7. Write summary.		X
8. Develop a matrix.		X

ments: assess the performance of each group, and assess each individual performance.

REVIEW AND PROVIDE ENRICHMENT AS NEEDED

The final task is to remediate and enrich student learning. First remediate the learning of students who were not completely successful. You should also develop an enrichment unit to extend the knowledge of those who did well.

A CONCLUDING NOTE

The discussion above and in the earlier chapters explains only one approach to using performance tasks to increase student learning. You should use all this information to develop your own system.

REFERENCES

Glatthorn, A. A. (1998). *Performance assessment and standards-based curricula.* Larchmont, NY: Eye on Education.

Kendall, J. S., & Marzano, R. J. (1997). *Content Guide.* Alexandria, VA: Association for Supervision and Curriculum Development.

13

LOOKING AHEAD TOWARD CONTINUED PROFESSIONAL GROWTH

Several factors suggest that teachers need to plan for their continued professional growth, especially with respect to curriculum, performance tasks, and performance assessment. The first factor is new research. The field is somewhat in a state of flux. It is a relatively new field, with researchers continuing to generate new knowledge. Yesterday's dogma may be tomorrow's obsolete idea. The second factor is new requirements. States and school districts will continue to develop new standards and tests that will impact directly on classroom teachers. The final factor is new knowledge from the field, as schools attempt to implement these new models. Already there are some indications that current curriculum standards are much too difficult and complex for many students. The discussion that follows suggests some guidelines for continued professional development for all teachers.

CONDUCT YOUR OWN RESEARCH

By this time, it has been well-established that classroom teachers can plan and conduct their own action research. (See Hubbard & Power, 1993, for a very useful handbook on action research methods.) Such classroom-generated knowledge fleshes out and complements the scholars' research. You should, of course, design your own action research; however, you may find the following example helpful.

- ◆ Organize a team of teacher-researchers. A team approach will probably be more effective than an individual project. Several school systems now permit experienced, competent teachers to use team research as a substitute for the standard teacher evaluation and supervision. (See Glatthorn, 1997, for several examples.) The team might be a grade-level team, a department, or just a group of volunteers.

♦ Identify a general area for investigation. Begin with a broad area, not a sharply defined research hypothesis. In the example here, the team might decide to study the general area of student attitudes toward performance assessments.

♦ Develop the knowledge base. In this critical step, the team uses the computer to search the knowledge base, so that it might know what others have learned. The Internet and the ERIC database are very useful resources.

♦ Define the research question you wish to answer. Based on the reading the team had done, the members decided to frame the research question this way:

> Do student attitudes towards performance assessments change over the course of the school year?

♦ Identify the inquiry methods you will use to answer the question. The methods can be several: survey; observation; interview; document analysis (such as grade reports, student journals, or test scores). In the example here, the team decided to survey students after the first performance assessments and after the last.

♦ Develop a schedule to carry out the research. Classroom research is time-consuming and should not be hurried—and a teacher's time is always in short supply. As the team examined its research project, the members decided to give the final survey in April, because teacher and student time is sharply limited in May and June.

♦ Implement the design flexibly, modifying it as the need arises.

◆ Disseminate your results by writing an article or entering your results on the Internet.

Other designs, of course, might be used. You may wish to start with a simpler approach.

GET FEEDBACK FROM YOUR STUDENTS

Even if you do not undertake an action-research project, you should still get feedback from your students. Obviously, you will monitor their performance throughout the project; but a post-unit assessment will also give you very useful results. Figure 13-1 is an example of a form that you might use. For the most part it uses students' language and a simple format. If you wish, you can figure the average answer for each question by assigning these values to each response: SA = 4; S = 3; D = 2; SD = 1. Most teachers find it helpful to supplement the survey with an informal discussion in class around the same issues.

FIGURE 13.1. STUDENT FEEDBACK FORM

To my students:

I can improve my teaching if you can answer frankly the following questions. Read the question and decide if you agree or disagree. Then circle one of these answers:

SA: strongly agree
A: agree
D: disagree
SD: strongly disagree

Your cooperation is much appreciated.

Statement	Your Answer
1. The unit was interesting to me.	SA A D SD
2. I learned a lot from this unit.	SA A D SD
3. The performance task was fun to do.	SA A D SD
4. The performance task helped me learn.	SA A D SD
5. The performance assessment was fair.	SA A D SD
6. The performance assessment helped me learn.	SA A D SD

Add Your Comments Below

INVITE A COLLEAGUE TO
OBSERVE YOUR TEACHING

Several experts in supervision, including this author, recommend that experienced, competent teachers should act as feedback sources to each other; such programs are referred to variously as *peer coaching, collegial observation,* and *peer supervision.* If such programs are seen only as a process of providing non-evaluative feedback, they tend to be effective. However, they should not become evaluative, because most teachers have negative feelings toward peer evaluation.

Many collegial feedback models are available. The one shown in Figure 13.2 has worked effectively with many faculties; a portion of the form has been completed just as an illustration.

It is based on the steps for implementing assessment-driven instruction. (See Figure 8.3, p. 113, and the accompanying text for additional information about the steps.)

Before using the form, stress with your colleague that you want objective feedback about what you did and how the students seemed to respond; you do not want evaluation.

PARTICIPATE IN STAFF-DEVELOPMENT WORKSHOPS

Staff-development workshops (sometimes called *in-service programs* can be very helpful if they are designed well and implemented effectively. If you can, provide leadership by ensuring that your school's staff-development programs follow the research-based guidelines shown in Figure 13.3 (p. 170). While those guidelines should be applied flexibly, they serve to remind you, your colleagues, and your principal what quality staff development programs should include.

ATTEND EXTERNAL WORKSHOPS AND ENROLL IN GRADUATE COURSES

As supplements to your school's workshops, consider attending external workshops, such as those sponsored by the professional organizations. The only caution here is that many such workshops report simply on positive anecdotal evidence: "All the teachers thought it was wonderful." Graduate courses

FIGURE 13.2. PEER FEEDBACK FORM

Step	Teacher Action	Student Work
1. Organizes Class	Gives overview; organizes class into 5 groups	Most seem attentive; 3 students in back seem off task
2. Engages Students		
3. Activates Prior Knowledge		
4. Facilitates Access to New Knowledge		
5. Facilitates Task Performance		
6. Conducts Performance Assessments		
7. Helps Students Represent Knowledge		
8. Provides Scaffolding		
9. Provides Formative Feedback		
10. Facilitates Metacognition		

**FIGURE 13.3. STAFF DEVELOPMENT GUIDELINES
(PARAPHRASED FROM SPARKS, 1995)**

According to the research, effective staff-development programs reflect these characteristics.

1. Maintain a focus on student learning.
2. Reflect the fact that change affects staff in personal ways.
3. Support and are related to changes in the school culture.
4. Involve a systems approach and are based on sound research.
5. Include content specific knowledge as well as pedagogical knowledge.
6. Use a teaching/learning process that models the type of instruction desired.
7. Emphasize job-embedded learning.
8. Provide for follow-up reinforcement and feedback.
9. Provide ample time for collaborative activities.

---

have their own limitations; many teachers find them too theoretical. However, both types of externally sponsored programs can help you stay up-to-date and extend your knowledge.

VISIT OTHER SCHOOLS

Many teachers find that visiting other schools and talking with teachers in those schools are the best ways of getting practical knowledge. If you do visit, be sure to make clear that the purpose of your visit is to learn, not to evaluate. Go with some specific questions to raise and take along the materials you have used successfully. Keep two cautions in mind when you visit. First, remember that you may be seeing a rehearsed classroom; students are usually on their best behavior for visitors. Also keep in mind that each school is different: what worked in the visited school may not work in yours.

READ, READ, AND READ

Despite the expanding technology, many teachers find that the best way to keep their knowledge current is to read widely. First, read new books as they are published. Eye on Education, the publisher of this book, has developed and continues to develop specialized strength in the fields of performance tasks and assessments. The reference section at the end of each chapter provides several leads. Also, read the professional journals and news weeklies. They provide very current information about this changing field. Finally, use the Internet to share what you have learned and to make contact with others.

REFERENCES

Glatthorn, A. A. (1997). *Differentiated supervision* (2nd ed.). Alexandria, VA: Association for Supervision and Curriculum Development.

Hubbard, R. S., & Power, B. M. (1993). *The art of classroom inquiry.* Portsmouth NH: Heinemann.

Sparks, D. (1995). Focusing staff development on improving student learning. In G. Cawelti (Ed.), *Handbook of research on improving student achievement* (pp. 163–169). Arlington, VA: Educational Research Service.

GLOSSARY

Achievement Cycle. The close interactive relationships of four elements: standards-based curricula; performance tasks and assessments; assessment-driven instruction; and authentic learning.

Assessment-Driven Instruction. Teaching and planning for teaching that are based on, derive from, and focus on performance tasks and assessments.

Assessment of Student Learning. The process of gathering data from multiple sources in order to make judgments about student learning.

Authentic Learning. Higher-order learning used in solving contextualized problems.

Benchmarks. Components of the standards, specifying expectations for a particular range of grades (such as 5-8) or a specific grade.

Classroom Learning Objectives. Specific learning outcomes derived from benchmarks, used to facilitate the classroom learning processes.

Content Benchmarks (usually identified as *benchmarks*). Components of content standards identified for a particular level of schooling or grade.

Content Standards. Statements of the skills and knowledge that students should learn in a given subject field by the end of their schooling (usually identified as *curriculum standards* or *standards*).

Curriculum Integration. Developing units of study that draw content from two or more subjects.

Curriculum Standards. Content standards.

Enrichment Units. Units developed to enrich, broaden, or deepen the required curriculum.

Generative Knowledge. Knowledge used in solving problems; contrast with *inert knowledge*, knowledge that is not used.

Instructional Teams. School-based groups of teachers at a given grade level or subject who are responsible for implementing the achievement cycle for their grade or subject.

Performance Assessment. Assessment that involves situations in which students must construct responses that illustrate their ability to apply knowledge.

Performance Standards. Indices of quality that specify how skilled or competent a student must be.

Performance Task. A complex open-ended problem posed for students to solve as a means of demonstrating mastery.

Performance -Task- and Performance-Assessment-Based Units. Organized sequence of lessons based and focused on the performance task and its related performance assessment.

Portfolio. An organized collection of artifacts that are assembled in order to demonstrate competency.

Rubrics. A guide for scoring assessments, usually specifying criteria and three to five standards of achievement.

Scaffolding. Support for learning, which is withdrawn gradually as students become able to work on their own.

Standards-Based Curricula. Curricula based on and derived from content standards.

Unit Scenario. Mental picture of the unit as it unfolds, which is envisioned to assist in the planning process.